Angel Animals

Exploring Our
Spiritual Connection
with Animals

Allen and Linda Anderson

Illustrations by Julie Johnson Olson

A PLUME BOOK

PLUME
Published by the Penguin Group
Penguin Putnam Inc., 375 Hudson Street, New York, New York 10014, U.S.A.
Penguin Books Ltd, 27 Wrights Lane, London W8 5TZ, England
Penguin Books Australia Ltd, Ringwood, Victoria, Australia
Penguin Books Canada Ltd, 10 Alcorn Avenue, Toronto, Ontario, Canada M4V 3B2
Penguin Books (N.Z.) Ltd, 182–190 Wairau Road, Auckland 10, New Zealand

Penguin Books Ltd, Registered Offices: Harmondsworth, Middlesex, England

First published by Plume, a member of Penguin Putnam Inc.

First Printing, September, 1999
10 9 8 7 6 5 4 3 2 1

"Angel Animals" is a registered trademark of William Allen Anderson.

Ⓟ REGISTERED TRADEMARK — MARCA REGISTRADA

LIBRARY OF CONGRESS CATALOGING-IN-PUBLICATION DATA
Angel Animals: exploring our spiritual connection with animals/
   [compiled by] Allen and Linda Anderson ; illustrations by Julie
   Johnson Olson.
      p.   cm.
   ISBN 0-452-28072-9
   1. Animals—Religious aspects.   2. Human-animal relationships.
I. Anderson, Allen, 1954– .   II. Anderson, Linda C., 1946– .
BL439.A53   1999
636.088'7—dc21   99-13700
                                                                 CIP

Printed in the United States of America
Set in Goudy and Birch
Designed by Eve L. Kirch

Angel Animals

"These stories show the beautiful and undeniable spiritual connection between people and animals."
—Kristin von Kreisler, author of *The Compassion of Animals*

"Brimming with firsthand accounts that lift your heart."
—Judy Guggenheim, coauthor of *Hello from Heaven!*

"Invites readers to rediscover and celebrate the spiritual unity between humans and animals. The wisdom within these pages will help people live healthier lives. It is as timely as it is stimulating and enlightening."
—Eleanor L. Harris, author of *Pet Loss: A Spiritual Guide*

"A joy to read! This treasure of a book delights, inspires, and adds to our growing understanding of the spiritual nature of animals."
—Stephanie Laland, author of *Peaceful Kingdom: Random Acts of Kindness by Animals*

"Reading this gentle book is like slipping through a secret door into a magical world where all creatures . . . are loved for their unique gifts . . . A beautiful book."
—Christine Davis, author of *For Every Dog an Angel*

"This book is pure joy! A terrific celebration of the enduring, deep and healing love between people and animals."
—Rosemary Ellen Guiley, author of *Prayer Works*

"An insightful, joy-filled, and exquisitely written book."
—Penelope Smith, author of *Animals . . . Our Return to Wholeness*

"This book is so wonderful because you remember some small encounter of your own, with a bird, a dragonfly, or a spider that changed your life." —Margot Lasher, author of *And the Animals Will Teach You*

Allen and Linda Anderson are cofounders of Angel Animals®, an organization devoted to raising awareness about the spiritual relationship between people and animals. Together, they are the editors of the *Angel Animals* newsletter, which invites animal lovers from around the world to share stories of how animals have enriched their lives. The Andersons live in Minneapolis with their family of angel animals.

Contents

Part One: What Angel Animals Teach Us About Relationships

Chapter One: Discovering Your Spiritual Connection with All Life

Chapter Two: Learning How to Love Unconditionally

Chapter Three: Creating Family Harmony

Chapter Four: Being Inspired to Pursue a Greater Good

**Part Two: What Angel Animals Teach Us About
Handling Life's Challenges**

Chapter Five: Sailing on the Winds of Change

Chapter Eight: Recognizing Life's Mystical Moments

Part Three: What Angel Animals Teach Us About Death, Dying, and the Afterlife

Chapter Nine: Saying Good-bye in Our Own Way

Chapter Ten: Going Through Grieving

Chapter Eleven: Messages from Heaven

Chapter Twelve: Recognizing Angel Animals Who Return

Acknowledgments

Our first thanks are to the animals who have blessed our lives with their loving presence. Truly our angels, they have been constant reminders that God loves us. We express gratitude to our current angel animals family: Taylor, Speedy, Cuddles, Sunshine, and Sparkle. To those animals who have shared our home and are now angels in heaven: Prana, Feisty, Mugsie, and Brandy. To the many angel animals who loved us while we were growing up under their vigilance and protection.

Deep appreciation to our families, especially to Bobbie Anderson, for her constant encouragement, and to Susan and Mun Anderson, our wonderful children.

Special thanks to Harold and Joan Klemp for helping us to see and hold the vision.

Our love and gratitude to the following:

All the people who contributed stories to this book and the magnificent angel animals who are the subjects of those stories. This book wouldn't exist without your generosity and the brightness of your light.

Arielle Ford and Brian Hilliard, of Dharma Dreams, our professional managers, who immediately caught the vision and helped us to realize it.

Parrel A. Caplan, an attorney, who helped us learn the process.

Jennifer Dickerson and Danielle Perez, our wonderful editors, who took us from the animal kingdom into the publishing kingdom.

Julie Johnson Olson, for her inspiring illustrations and stories.

Marty Becker, D.V.M., for his beautiful foreword and for inspiring us with "the Bond."

Special gratitude to all the people who endorsed the book.

For early support of this project, we especially thank the following people: Barbara Buckner, Jane Angus, Carol Frysinger, David and Catherine Purnell, Diane Sorenson, Peter and Patti Lucchese, Debbie Johnson, Myron Cheshaek, April Munson, Diane Sterling, Cheng Yew Chung, Giovanni and Liz Riva, Stephen and Liz Mallett, Joann Marie Donahoe, D.V.M., Victoria Bullis, Peter and Sheri Skelskey, Sharon and Doug Kunin, Ilona Goin, John Kulick, Catherine Kirk Chase, Lawrence Chase, Ann Archer, Alden Butcher, Kristy Walker, Garrick Colwell, Diana and Henry Stewart-Koster, Linda Lansdell, Maureen Dixon, Margo Hendricks, Jack Heyl, Mary Carroll Moore, Anthony Moore, Bettine Clemen, Peter Longley, Olinda Floro, Lynn LaFroth, Lynn Schultz, Debbie Luican and Learning Annex, Claudie Courdevault, Bob and Suzanne Hayes, John Lindsay, Laurence Cruz, Jan Warren, Sheila Sudit, Stephanie Laland, Margot Lasher, Douglas Rubel at Safari, Ltd., Lori Peterson, Brad Woodard, Molly Guthrey, Martha Sawyer Allen, Teri Keish, Lynn Harper, and Charles Richards.

Foreword

When pets and people live in interdependence and harmony, all of life is enriched. That's the core meaning of "the Bond," a term I coined to describe this special connection and to bring attention to the joys and rewards of human–animal relationships.

We share this small planet with all of God's creatures and all of us have a tremendous will to live. Rather than thinking of ourselves as being superior to animals, increasingly we are seeing them as teachers, healers, angels, and friends . . . for individuals, families, communities, and society.

Animals have their own ways, languages, and methods of communication. Perhaps we're beginning to understand them better after centuries of living together. Or maybe we understood long ago, forgot, and are now gradually remembering our deeper connections. For millions of us, the animals' messages come across loud and clear if we can only open ourselves up to receive them.

We've always known that animals make us feel good. Today, scientific proof is backing up living-room logic to show that they are actually good for our health. And now, this book, *Angel Animals: Exploring Our Spiritual Connection with Animals*, spotlights the spiritual joys and rewards of sharing our lives with animals. *Angel Animals* is a wonderful tapestry of stories illuminating the miracles of "the Bond." From a three-legged dog teaching an abused woman how to forgive, to dolphins compassionately rescuing a swimmer from drowning at sea or a cat gently resolving family arguments, this incredible collection of stories puts an enlightening and energizing light on how animals enrich and lengthen our lives with their spiritual gifts. For many of us who witness the loving hand of God manifest itself through His many creatures, it is clear that they are indeed angels.

Allen and Linda Anderson's book offers inspiration and insight into rediscovering or receiving the ancient spiritual connections between mankind and the rest of the animal kingdom. After a relentless search, the Andersons have assembled a collection of extraordinary stories from ordinary people around the globe. Besides inspiring you, the authors go a step further by highlighting practical, daily life benefits embedded in the stories, such as how animals expand our circle of concern, improve our relationships, love us unconditionally, help us to handle life's inevitable upsets, and aid us in dealing with loss and grief. The points and principles that the Andersons bring to their readers' attention show that "angel animals"—a term they have introduced—help us to create better lives for ourselves and perhaps, more importantly, for others. Never preachy, the book focuses on how animals naturally use spiritual principles and encourages readers to draw their own conclusions and life lessons, and to find the parallels in their lives.

The subjects of the stories in this book represent a cross section of the ark—dogs, cats, horses, fish, raccoons, deer, insects, rodents, reptiles, bears—you name it. In heartwarming, dramatic, and irrefutable ways they demonstrate that by celebrating, protecting, nurturing, and sharing "the Bond" with our beloved pets and all animals, we move further along the road toward acquiring the desired spiritual traits of graciousness, kindness, unconditional love, loyalty, generosity, and inner peace.

Reading about "angel animals" in this book and reflecting upon the positive and profound lessons they can provide to us, if we let them, helps satisfy a deep, primal spiritual hunger. This book delivers to readers—all of us who are caught in this modern high-tech, low-touch world, with its disguises, pressures, and hectic pace—the most angelic and simplest of messages: We are all God's creatures and His Creation is the classroom of the wise.

If we open our eyes like children and see beyond the limits of the human world to the synergies of the animal world, our basic human requirements—to be loved, to need and be needed—are fulfilled beyond our wildest imaginings. And miracles are not just possible but probable.

—Marty Becker, D.V.M.
Coauthor, *Chicken Soup for the Pet Lover's Soul*™

Introduction

One spring day we walked around the lake near our house. Our dog Taylor pranced in front of us with a big grin that made passersby smile at her exuberance. We were talking about the valuable life lessons we were learning from animals and beloved pets. As a cool Minnesota breeze filtered through the trees, we realized that animals, as a bonus to the endless supply of love and joy they've brought to our lives, were teaching us valuable spiritual lessons. Excitedly, we began to list the many ways these special creatures with whom we'd shared our home over the years were teaching us about love, mercy, and inner peace.

Now, we'd like to invite you on that walk with us. So, first we'd like to introduce you to each member of our family.

After our two wonderful children were grown, we filled our empty nest with pets. Three of them—Mugsie, a cat with an attitude who lived twenty-one years; Prana, a gentle golden retriever who taught us the meaning of service; and Feisty, pure love in a cat's body—are no longer with us physically, but they live on in our hearts and memories. Now, meet our current family.

The Anderson Angel Animal Kingdom

Taylor, our yellow Labrador retriever, is a bundle of boundless energy. We named her Taylor as a play on words because her puppy dog tail wagged with such force that it sometimes knocked her over. Filled with a zest for life, she's inexhaustible. Taylor runs through the field behind our house with wild abandon, ears flapping, leaping through the air as if she were flying on angel wings.

Speedy, a brown and gray tabby with a tiny face, is our resident scaredy-cat. We rescued Speedy, the last of a litter, from a house where the toddler confused him with a Ninja warrior and attempted to strangle him. When we met him, the kitten flung himself over Linda's shoulder, purred like a freight train, and yelled, "Get me out of here!" Since then, he's become more trusting and affectionate. He often wraps himself around Linda's legs at night and sleeps curled up between us.

Sunshine and Sparkle are two lively, personable cockatiels. This daring duo come out of their cage when the other animals are safely tucked away. They live courageously in a houseful of natural predators.

Sparkle, a gray female with light orange circles on her cheeks and streaks of yellow feathers, is the quieter of the two birds. But she is an adventurer, always the first to explore new territory. Sparkle sits on our heads to groom our hair and she nibbles crumbs from our breakfast plates. She massages Sunshine's neck with her beak when he settles down and stops chasing her.

Sunshine, bright yellow with lustrous orange circles like spots of rouge on his cheeks, is the sound master of the family. He melts our hearts by saying, "I love you, Sweet Baby," followed by birdie kisses. He serenades us with birdsongs he hears in the neighborhood, his rendition of "This Old Man," plus a variety of whistles and chirps. He sounds like the telephone ringing when he wants attention or needs a good laugh as we run to answer it/him. He makes the sound of the cellular phone when he considers the situation to be an emergency. When he finishes

ringing, he often says, "Hello." Sunshine, whose favorite letter
seems to be Z, uses his beak to help Allen type at the computer
keyboard.

The newest addition to our family is Cuddles, a black kitten
with white on her paws, belly, whiskers, and the tip of her nose.
One of her back legs is white on the outside and the other is
white on the inside making her look as if she'd been dipped in a
paint bucket by an absentminded artist. No matter where Cuddles is in the house, the kitty often runs to sit on Linda's lap
while she takes time each morning for prayer and quiet reflection. Cuddles has been teaching us how to get in touch with our
"inner kitten." She's shown us that no matter how serious things
might be, anything can be turned into a toy, and we've learned
from her that it's really fun to chase your tail.

We Wondered What Was Happening with Others

You've just met the coauthors of the unique book you're about
to read that was spawned after that spring afternoon walk. After
all our discussion, we began to wonder if other people were discovering their spiritual connection with animals.

A project started taking shape in our imaginations. Allen
sent a request to pet publications and animal organizations asking if people wanted to share stories about the spiritual truths
and lessons animals teach us. He posted flyers on local bulletin
boards. He also went on the Internet and placed an announce-
ment in pet and animal interest groups. Within thirty days,
we received over one hundred replies. Ordinary people from
all over the world wrote about their spiritual experiences with
dogs, cats, raccoons, chickens, rabbits, horses, rodents, and birds.
Their quality stories were touching, humorous, and remarkably
inspiring.

Now, as two writers, we discussed how we could share the stories we were collecting. They were too wonderful to keep to ourselves. We decided to publish a newsletter and call it *Angel*

Animals. Within months, we'd established a web site, thousands of people from many countries had asked for more information, the publication was mentioned favorably in magazines and newspapers, and we were doing interviews, workshops and presentations. We were on our way to sharing stories from people just like us who have realized that their neighborhoods, backyards, parks, and skies are teeming with conscious life.

We defined angel animals by going back to the Greek derivation for the word *angel*, which is *angelos* and literally means *messenger*. Angel animals are messengers. They assure us that God's love, guidance, and protection are near all the time.

Angel animals are daily companions or creatures we observe in nature. They naturally demonstrate spiritual qualities such as gratitude, survival, courage, and forgiveness. They connect us to our higher nature because they operate from their higher nature; beyond thought and emotion, they love unconditionally. If we hear the spiritual messages angel animals send, we'll improve our relationships, our ability to handle life's challenges, and increase our understanding of the spiritual realms.

What Is the Nature of Animals?

To bring the concept of angel animals into the world, we began to research books about animals. We found that a debate raged in some of them and often consumed pages of text. Authors expressed concern or offered arguments to prove that their observations about animals were not merely anthropomorphic (can anybody actually pronounce that word?) behavior.

Since we're not scientists or animal experts, we don't feel compelled to worry about losing credibility with our esteemed colleagues. In a moment of true confession, we asked ourselves if we were being anthropomorphic—attributing human characteristics such as thoughts, feelings, and states of consciousness onto animals. The answer was, as they say in Minnesota, "You betcha!" And proud of it, we might add.

But in writing this book, we're not limiting animals to mere reflections of human behavior. In the stories we've collected and are sharing with readers, animals use logic. They strategize. They feel. They remember and interpret. They make choices. Skeptics might dismiss the incredible aspects of any one of these stories as mere coincidence. But because we've received so many stories and read hundreds of others, the volume of anecdotes and examples, combined with our own experiences have led us to view animals as conscious spiritual beings with spiritual natures. We believe that animals, rather than trying to imitate human behavior, view life in their own unique ways from perspectives that are as low as our ankles, as high as the sky, and as expansive as eternity.

We're neither theologians nor philosophers, so we don't feel the need to present arguments about whether or not animals have souls, go to heaven, or return after death in miraculous ways to comfort the loved ones they left behind. Some authors in this book seem to believe all of these things about animals and others don't believe much or any of it. Their stories often raise more questions than they answer.

But again, we're content to accept the proof of our own experiences. We've seen that animals are complex characters. Just as humans have a spiritual dimension in addition to mental, emotional, and physical aspects, so do animals. We've observed that animals—rather than being saintlike—act as humans do, from the level of base instinct all the way up the scale to displaying spiritual virtues. Yet, it's remarkable to us how often animals choose higher versus lower paths. We marvel at how many animals are naturally compassionate and forgiving, for example, instead of clinging to fear, anger, and mistrust.

We know, as do many people who live with animals, that animals enrich our lives spiritually. We've made a point in this book of mentioning possibilities to consider rather than preaching about what people should or shouldn't believe. Even though some churches invite animals to their worship services (Linda had a funny moment in Africa with a chicken who regularly attends the worship services), animals don't belong exclusively to one religion or another. Angel animals show us how to be truly religious by tuning in to our spiritual essence and acting as carriers of God's love into this world.

Mystical animal images grace Ice Age caves. From earliest times, dogs have been our companions. Of course, cats wait with dignity to be restored to their rightful pedestals and worshiped as the deities they were in ancient Egypt. Artists depict humans flying on winged horses. Since the dawn of civilization, humans have known what many today are rediscovering: *When we look into the eyes of an angel animal, we see their spiritual natures. We see ourselves reflected in their gentle gaze. We see the work of a loving God.*

How We've Written This Book

We've selected stories that have what we call the "chill factor." When we read them, they made a chill run up our spines. It was hard to choose and we had to leave out some remarkable stories because there just wasn't enough space for all of them. The ones we're sharing with you are unique, inspiring, and amazing. They tell about a variety of animals demonstrating important spiritual principles. Most of the people who wrote to us aren't professional writers and their stories have never been published. The storytellers come from many walks of life, cultures, parts of the world, and belief systems. Before each story, we've told you a little about the author and the important angel animals in their lives. We encourage you to look in the back of the book, in the section "More About the Authors," for additional information about them.

The book is organized into three parts with twelve chapters. Each part introduces ways that spiritually connecting with animals improves the quality of our lives. Introductory and closing material contains shorter stories on each chapter's theme. In between the introduction and closing sections of each chapter are a series of intriguing longer stories told in the first person by the authors.

When we edited each precious story, we kept the animal's viewpoint in mind. We asked the question, *What is the spiritual message this angel animal is trying to deliver?* So, after the longer stories, we added some points to reflect upon. These afterthoughts present life lessons that the angel animals in each story may be teaching. If you're wondering what makes *Angel Animals* different from other collections of inspiring stories about animals, the afterthought is one of this book's unique features. It's a tool to help you look at the stories in relation to your own life. To focus the afterthought, we asked each contributor, "What did you learn from your experience with an angel animal?" The afterthoughts are designed to help you extend the stories from the abstract and inspirational to the practical and beneficial.

If angel animals are messengers to help us connect to our higher natures and to all life, then it makes sense to take a look at what they're doing. Whenever we're trying to understand situations in our own lives, we often ask each other, for example, "How would Taylor, Cuddles, Speedy, Sunshine, or Sparkle handle this situation?" Each animal in our family offers a unique perspective. We've found that by observing how angel animals reflect our thoughts and actions back to us, we learn volumes. If we overlook the wealth of wisdom and insight angel animals have to share, it's like living in a room full of encyclopedias without ever referring to them. We're forgetting to open our gifts from God, when we ignore what angel animals are teaching us. Angel animals show us how we're all connected by the golden thread of the Creator's love.

We Invite You to Join Us in the Exploration

As you read and reflect on the stories in this book, we invite you to explore the following questions with us:

- Have animals, as our spiritual partners, learned things that humans aren't aware of yet?
- What do animals experience that humans can't?
- Are angel animals helping us in amazing ways?
- Would it help humans to understand and emulate spiritual virtues that animals demonstrate?
- Why are angel animals in your life? Do they have a spiritual purpose for being with you?
- Are angel animals delivering spiritual messages? What are they?

At the end of the book, we've told you more about ourselves, other Angel Animals projects, and how you can get in touch with us. We're always collecting more angel animals stories and would love to hear from you.

A heartfelt wish, from our family to yours, is that after you've read these stories and thought about spiritual lessons you're learning from angel animals, you'll view the creatures with whom we share this planet in a whole new light.

The light of God.

—Allen and Linda Anderson

Part One

WHAT ANGEL ANIMALS TEACH US ABOUT RELATIONSHIPS

Animals offer tremendous help by simply being who and what they are. They are beings who still remember the original instructions given them by an ancient universe.

—Susan Chernak McElroy

Our deepest connection with animals is spiritual.

It's true that animals offer emotional comfort and practical assistance. But talk to those who have been transported to a heavenly place by the gentle purring of a kitten or whose broken hearts, burdened by care and pain, have been mended by a dog licking their hand. They'll tell you that angel animals connect us with the River of Life in ways poets imagine and mystics contemplate.

We believe that humans and animals share their lives spiritually as well as physically.

Some belief systems teach that before we begin our earthly existence souls are guided by God, Spirit, the Creator, the Divine, the Sacred—whatever your word is for the Source of all life—into exactly the body, mind, emotions, and circumstances that will help us grow spiritually.

Have animals also made agreements with life?

Do animals gain spiritual experience in this earthly classroom using bodies that walk, crawl, hop, slither, fly, or leap? Did animals, for spiritual reasons, accept positions in the circle of life?

The angel animals you're going to meet in part one may help you answer these fundamental questions about life or reinforce truths you already know in your heart.

Angel Animals Teach Spiritual Lessons About Relationships

In part one, you'll explore how animals—viewing and relating to the world in their unique ways—teach spiritual lessons about relationships. The stories in part one demonstrate that angel animals help us discover our essential connection with creation, find hidden pockets of love in everyday life, bring families together, and inspire us to greatness.

If you wish, reflect on and apply the spiritual lessons embedded in each story. We hope that the stories and afterthoughts will help you to deepen your spiritual connection with people, animals, and all life.

Chapter One

Discovering Your Spiritual Connection with All Life

johnson

Ask the sea gulls offshore
The time of the tide.
"We're leaving," they'll answer,
"So, ask the waves!"

—Japanese Zen saying

ach morning, when we take the cover off our cockatiels' cage to welcome the day, Sunshine's first words to us and his wife, Sparkle, are, "I love you, Sweet Baby." This bird has an extensive vocabulary of words, whistles, and songs. But he chooses to assure us that we're loved by our birds, by the universe, by God.

Spiritual connections are illuminated in many other ways by the angel animals in our home. If one of us is away, we always know when the other is returning because our dog, Taylor, linked to us in ways that sometimes seem unfathomable, always sits alertly at the window or door about five minutes before the missing person's arrival. She reminds us that we are drawn together through invisible, golden strands of mutual love.

Recognizing Your Spiritual Connection with All Life

Many people have written to us about how they've recognized the sacred connections between themselves and angel animals or even insects. In "Healing with a Dragonfly," Kathia Haug Thal-mann, a professional language translator from Switzerland, writes, "So many times God has spoken to me about love through ani-mals. I was sitting in a very powerful spiritual place outdoors and could feel this healing energy. I asked God to help me heal from an inner wound. In that instant, a beautiful dragonfly with golden wings landed in the palm of my open hand and stayed there for a long time. This immediately opened my heart to re-ceive the healing. I cried tears of joy."

If you accept that your very essence is gently woven into the arch of a rainbow, the lap of a wave upon the shore, and the wag-ging of a puppy dog's tail, then you'll be filled with the spiritual virtue of abundance. You'll know that love and miracles are all around. If only you can recognize and accept them, you'll under-stand the message of angel animals.

The chapter you're about to read will introduce angel animals who show us the reality and importance of our connections with all creation. They make us aware of our spiritual lifelines to each other and to God.

Juan Antonio, his wife, Maria, and their two children enjoy life with their dachshunds, Tatú and Winnie, in Cuernavaca, Morelos, Mexico. Juan is an ordained minister and a body therapist. He volunteers as a translator and fulfills a leadership role in his church. A dream showed his ancient connections with the animal kingdom.

Angel Animals Taught Me Ancient Secrets

JUAN ANTONIO SANTESTEBAN

After reading the *Angel Animals* newsletter, I had a most interesting dream.

I gradually realized that I was dreaming of floating on the ocean. The completely still air and water glowed with a light blue and golden mist. As I became more aware of my surroundings, I realized that I was holding on to something that seemed to keep me afloat. In this dream, I knew there was a spiritual guide nearby. He was busy looking after some sea animals who needed his help.

As I slowly gained awareness in the dream, I felt and could see more clearly the flat yellow surface that gave support to my left arm. It was about three feet long and looked like a small surfboard. It helped to keep me buoyant in a very gentle way.

Finally, it dawned on me. My support was a fish! Even though it remained perfectly still, I began to feel its gentle life pulses. I sensed a sweet flow of love emanating from it.

Then I discovered that there was a smaller purple fish holding up and leading my right hand in a flowing dance under the water.

As I moved with it, I tried not to disturb my quieter companion, the yellow fish.

At this moment, I had an astounding insight. The fish were teaching me that this was the kind of friendship—loving and full of trust—that we enjoyed with other life-forms a long time ago.

Later in the dream, I talked with the spiritual guide whom I had seen helping the fish earlier—a young fellow who evidently enjoyed giving service to the ocean's creatures. I was reminded of all the spiritual beings, the angels who work with us and creation so we can realize more of God's love. I felt grateful for their self-less service and remembered that we can all be angels for each other.

Fins to Flap: Have you ever had a dream about an animal that helped you gain deeper insight? Has an angel animal shown you the ancient, deep connections animals and humans have had in the past? Would you like to try writing down your dreams in a journal? Pay special attention to those in which angel animals visit and whisper secrets of how and where to find love.

Karen is a doctor in alternative medicine from Calgary, Alberta, Canada. Through personal experience and her patients' stories, she has learned of the many ways our connections with angel animals help us to heal.

Kitty Connected Me to the Healing Power of Love

KAREN JENSEN, N.D.

I was entering the homestretch of my internship at the naturopathic medical college with all the symptoms of burnout. My graduation requirements would be met well ahead of schedule, so I could have some time with my children. My body had been warning me to slow down for months, but I really wanted some time with my kids before exams so I didn't listen. One day a friend dropped by and pried me away from my studies, insisting that we go cycling. On the trail in front of me was a young man pedaling at quite a clip. My inner voice warned me to slow down because he didn't realize that I was behind him. But as I'd been doing in the rest of my life lately, I ignored the signals. The cyclist stopped suddenly. Soon I was airborne, flying over both bikes. I came down hard on the pavement and landed on my hip.

At first, the incredible piercing pain made it impossible for me to talk or to open my eyes. A crowd gathered around me. I insisted that I didn't need to go to the hospital and, after being taken home, I was still in denial about the seriousness of my fall. Later that day, I asked the X-ray instructor at my school to take films of my pelvis. He confirmed what I'd been afraid to accept—I was severely injured. The reality of the situation flooded in. I wouldn't be able to complete my final school year and graduate. My plans to begin practicing as a health care professional would be ruined. And I had barely enough money to support my children. The healing process for a broken hip joint and pubic bone would take months.

With the help of this big, gruff X-ray instructor, who suddenly transformed into a gentle soft-spoken man, I began to realize that somehow I'd survive this setback. However, it was time to go home and feel sorry for myself, which I managed to do very well for a day or so. Then in the midst of all the pain, I caught a glimpse of the valuable opportunity this experience could provide. I came to the realization that this injury would bring lessons and spiritual growth beyond my wildest imagination. My attitude changed. Suddenly I was filled with the most heartfelt love and gratitude. The next morning my pain was gone, but the long healing journey still loomed ahead.

A Kitten Named Kitty Helped Me Fulfill My Dream

Right around the time of my accident, our cat had a litter of kittens. I found good homes for all but one, the runt who wasn't very cute; in fact, he was a downright ugly kitten. As a single parent of three young children who was attending medical school full-time, I didn't want any more responsibility, but I also didn't have the heart to give the kitten to the pound. It was only after I was injured that I discovered this little kitten, whom we named Kitty, would prove vital to me.

While I lay flat on my back in bed over the long days of recovery, Kitty would purr as loudly as he could. Somehow he seemed to know where my bone was broken and he'd lie directly on that spot. I never placed him in this position. He just found the injury by himself and covered it with his body. Sometimes he purred so loudly that my son had to take him out of the room, so I could get some sleep. This little healing machine continued to drape his tiny body over the broken bone and purr, emitting waves of love, day in and day out for weeks.

About five weeks after the accident, I just sensed that the break had healed. I went to my X-ray instructor and asked him to take new films. He assured me that it was impossible for new bone to form in such a short time. I told him to humor me, so he did. When he examined the X-rays, he shook his head and said, "I don't know what you've been doing, but whatever it is, you're healed enough to use your crutches, very carefully."

I thought back to Kitty and I smiled at the miracle and blessing this little creature had brought about in my life. Because of his love, I'd be able to finish school in record time, support my family, and fulfill my dream of practicing naturopathic medicine.

One cold November morning I was leaving the house for my first day back at school. Kitty raced out in front of me and decided to play a game of "come and find me if you can." Because I didn't dare risk injuring myself by falling on the ice, I decided not to chase him, but asked the children to bring him back inside. They searched everywhere, but couldn't find him. By that evening we had asked all the neighbors, but no one had seen him. On the second day of Kitty's absence, a neighbor told us that she'd seen him get run over by a truck. I was absolutely devastated and the mother cat's heart was also broken.

Why had this untimely death happened to an innocent creature who had given so much of himself to help me?

Later, I reflected on how my connection with this loving animal had been a sacred one. Is it possible, I wondered, that he'd come into this life with a special purpose? Had he helped me through the painful times, opening my heart to the miracles that love can bring, and then left this earth with his mission completed? I realized that he'd taught me one of life's most important lessons—my hardest experiences are often the greatest opportunities for growth.

A Paw to Lick: Does Kitty demonstrate the power of love to heal and how meaningful a life can be, even if it's short? To explore your connection with all life, is there a person or animal you know who could use a little "purring"—some encouraging words? Does someone have a spot of suffering that you could ease with loving attention?

Anne is a naturalist, artist, and healer from Portland, Oregon, who helps people to reconnect spiritually to nature, a subject she's writing a book about. Her special buddy is C.J., a cat who she says is quite a wise and wonderful friend. An angel animal bird gave Anne a new perspective on gardening.

A Bird's Message About the Importance of Mustard Seeds

ANNE CEDERBERG

It was a wonderful morning in the garden. I'd weeded and was ready to leave, but weeding seemed unrewarding. I wanted something fun to bring home. I saw the mustard plants, which had all formed seeds, and wondered if they were ready to harvest.

I walked over to get a closer look. It was too early to harvest the seeds, I thought. The lower pods had not only turned brown but had shed their seeds. They seemed to have been gnawed at, as though an insect or something had been eating them.

Should I pull up the mustard plants? There were so many. What could I do with so much seed, a big enough supply for years to come? While I pondered what to do, a bird flew within an inch of my forearm as if he were going to land on me. The bird fluttered to about a foot in front of me and hovered. In midair, he turned to look at me. I flinched, startled by his closeness. In response, he flinched too and flew to a nearby branch.

After he perched on the tree, the bird immediately looked at me. I greeted him, telling him how beautiful he was and that I felt honored to be treated like a natural landing pad!

The bird flew to another stake nearby. Again, he turned and looked at me, his red-violet breast and plumage glowing like a jewel in the midday sun. Then he soared to a neighbor's garden, where the mustard plants were in an earlier, flowering stage. He landed on one of the delicate plants, yet barely bent it. The bird looked at me and began to hop around on the plant top. He'd try to eat the seeds, then look at me, and try again. He wasn't having much luck because the seeds weren't developed.

Suddenly, I got the message!

The birds need and want seeds from my mustard plants. One of them came as a great messenger to let me know that the garden wasn't only for me and that I'd been looking at it only from a human's perspective. Needless to say, all the mustard plants with their seedpods remained! The bird messenger taught me that I don't know all the mysterious interactions happening in my garden. A little bird helped me to trust that everything has a purpose, whether I understand it or not.

Wings to Fly: Are angel animals in your own backyard trying to deliver messages that this earth with its bounty isn't here only for us?

Mary Elizabeth is from South Bend, Indiana. Her avocations include writing, women's health issues, gerontology, spirituality, and family memoirs. She has a Ph.D. in psychology/administration from the University of Notre Dame and is retired from her profession as a college professor and administrator. She shares a story about how she discovered, during her time of grief, that she had more in common with an angel animal than she ever imagined.

Sharing Grief with Joey

M. E. MARTUCCI, PH.D.

Joey, a light brown cocker spaniel, had been abandoned. My friend Katy was on duty as a vet technician the day Joey was brought in. It was love at first sight for both of them, but there were major problems: Katy already had two dogs. What to do?

A week passed with Katy singing the praises of Joey. His bright, black eyes, beautiful disposition, and youthful playfulness made the decision about his future a dilemma. Finally, Katy had a solution. Her daughter's birthday was the following month. What greater gift for a woman living alone than to receive a dog like Joey? Luckily, Katy's daughter shared her mom's love of animals and Joey's fate was sealed.

Though Joey loved his new home and his new human companion, when Katy visited her daughter, the first ten minutes were pure chaos. Joey jumped and ran, sat on Katy's lap, licked her face, and, finally, rested at her feet. The original bond between them remained intact. Katy's commands and wishes for the dog always superseded her daughter's.

Joey and Katy Reunited

Two years passed and Katy became seriously ill. Following surgery, chemotherapy, and extended treatments, Katy's condition became terminal. She moved in with her daughter for the final phase of her life.

Joey was delighted to have his old friend there even though he had to take a backseat to her care and treatment. When Katy was alert and feeling stronger, she touched Joey and communicated with him in their special way. Joey never went far from her bedside, spending hours under Katy's bed and, occasionally, standing up to look at her. It was touching to watch as he'd lick her hands through the bed rails.

As Katy's condition worsened, her husband often took Joey away for a few days. This routine was followed for weeks with no one being concerned about Joey or his response to what was going on with Katy. In fact, it became a bit of a nuisance having Joey around those last days after Katy went into a coma and required more diligent care. We humans, of course, knew what the outcome had to be, but we failed to read the signs. We didn't want to face reality, I suppose. Even the health care professionals would only speculate about how much time Katy still had to live.

But Joey knew.

Joey Announced Katy's Condition

One day Joey returned to the house after being away for several nights. The dog could hardly wait for the door to be opened. He scratched furiously as the key was inserted. When the door opened slightly, he broke from his lead, squealing loudly as if he were injured. He ran to Katy's room.

Joey frantically began running around and under the bed in a way that wasn't how he usually acted when excited. I tried to quiet him, but he wouldn't calm down. Finally, sensing his dismay, I began to speak softly and gently to the dog. I told him that everything was all right. He stopped running, sat upright, looked at me, and wailed. His cries were so heart-wrenching that the other family members came to the door, thinking that I was the one who was crying.

Joey continued to wail for a few more minutes as he glanced up at Katy. I thought of letting Joey sit on the chair beside the bed. He immediately jumped on it and looked at Katy's face. He moaned less loudly. Katy's hand was outside the covers at her side. Joey leaned over to lick it. Gently moaning and watching Katy's face for some response, Joey stayed by her side while I spoke words of consolation. I wasn't sure if my tears were for my dying friend or a reaction to Joey's expression of grief.

Until then, I didn't think death was imminent. Nor did I realize that pets also grieve the loss of loved ones. Does God provide consolation for animals? I thought. Who helps them work through their grief? Then I remembered Saint Francis, the patron saint of animals. He seemed to have had some answers. I wondered if humans today could learn from studying this gentle saint's love and understanding for all God's creatures.

After a while, Joey quieted down, taking his usual place under the bed. He never left the room even for his daily walk and refused to eat. In a strange way, Joey was a source of comfort and a healing presence for me as I kept vigil and prayed.

Later that evening, Katy died. Joey was quiet. He stayed out of our way as we attended to Katy. When we called him to leave the apartment, Joey walked solemnly out the door. He seemed to know that Katy's life on this earth was over.

It's been said that sorrow creates a gaping hole inside that can later be filled with love. Meanwhile, life goes on, until one day, after some internal timetable has been satisfied, we are once again whole. Often we find ourselves with a greater capacity for compassion, patience, and understanding following our period of grief. Joey taught me that something similar happens in pets. When I recall the experience, as I continue to heal, I'm reminded that we humans have more in common with animals than we'd like to think. Let us hope we can celebrate the things we share with animals, such as the ability to love, to grieve, and to heal, and seek to learn from them.

> **A Tail to Wag:** Are angel animals so connected with us that they share our losses? Is their loyalty, devotion, and compassion an example of how to console others who are suffering?

Ray is a writer, cartoonist, and illustrator who lives in Tucson, Arizona. His experience involves a baby seal, a rainbow, and a love song.

A Baby Seal Helped Me See Our Divine Connection

RAY McBRIDE

My task was a simple one. Descend the steps to the beach, walk to where the seal was reported to be resting, and guard him from those who might touch or harm him. Seal pups, like most newborns, are loving and completely trusting. This makes them quite susceptible to people's overconcern and affection. Human handling can result in the baby seal being tragically abandoned.

My wife called the Marine Sciences Center in Newport, Oregon, while I waited for someone to come with warning signs to post around the seal pup. Watching closely, I felt the love of Spirit flowing from this small, delicate form that stretched and yawned beneath the warm rays of the sun.

Advancing as closely as I dared, I began to softly sing HU, an ancient love song to the Creator. This is a sacred name for God that I'd learned connects us spiritually with all life. As I sang with my eyes closed and love in my heart, I suddenly felt the impulse to look at the newborn creature. His ebony eyes reflected the bottomless depths of soul. I knew in that instant that our hearts were singing the same song.

Sensing that I should now give the seal pup plenty of space, yet stay close enough to protect him, I moved to a rock some sixty feet away. I sat waiting, then turned to look down the beach. I was presented with a sign of great beauty as a divine presence greeted me. Directly overhead, a small rainbow had appeared. Unlike the usual arch, this rather short rainbow lay straight and parallel. It displayed its radiant spectrum for only a minute and then faded from my view. In a moment, the message that life had delivered was clear: *Only love is real.*

On that day, a small seal pup had opened my heart to a deeper connection and love for all creation.

A Wave to Ride: Would you like to sing HU, OM, God, Holy Spirit, Jesus, Allah, or your own sacred name for God to an animal? If so, close your eyes, become quiet and peaceful, take a deep breath, fill yourself with love, and sing a holy name for God. Feel your sacred connection with all God's creatures.

Bill and his wife, Helen, have lived in Olympia, Washington, for twenty-eight years and in that time have opened their home to fifteen cats whom they describe as "all friends and all different." Their current cats are Velvet, L.G., and Arnold. Bill is a retired social worker and now enjoys volunteering for his church and a hospice organization. Bill's story is about how asking angel animals to assist us can reveal how spiritually connected we are with them.

Bigfoot Used Her Big Foot to Help Me

Bill Hodgson

Bigfoot came to my wife and me from a relative who raised Siamese cats. Her right rear foot was injured at an early age and even though our veterinarian did all he could, it remained three times as large as the others. A Siamese with this deformity isn't salable, so we adopted Bigfoot into our family of previously homeless cats.

Bigfoot soon replaced her typical Siamese yowls with the softer mews of our other cats. After graduating from kittenhood, Bigfoot quickly became the head of the household.

Bigfoot lived with us for many years and amazed us with her antics. However, her most memorable act occurred when I was ready to leave for an important seminar. With only one hour before departure, I realized that my airline ticket wasn't in the place where I usually kept such things.

Help!

I spent the next half hour frantically looking for the ticket all through the house. Bigfoot stayed with me and watched me quizzically. It was as if she were saying, "You sure are acting strange today." I became increasingly worried. My ticket was nowhere in sight.

I'd reached the end of my patience. With all the frustration I felt by then, I asked out loud, "Bigfoot, Bigfoot, where is my ticket?"

The cat immediately leaped up five feet to a shelf in my office. She deliberately used her big foot to dislodge a pile of papers and topple them. There, in the middle of the papers, on the floor, was my ticket.

I grabbed the ticket and headed for the door, only stopping to look back once and say, "Thank you, Bigfoot."

She looked at me and seemed to say, "Well, if you'd told me what you were looking for, I'd have helped you find it sooner!"

A Paw to Lick: Next time you're in trouble, test out your spiritual connection with an angel animal by asking him or her to help you. And, please, let us know what happens!

Some Final Connections

Sometimes, before people do extraordinary things with their lives, they have a miraculous connection with an angel animal. In *First Dogs: American Presidents and Their Best Friends*, a wonderful book by Roy Rowan and Brooke Janis, the authors tell a story about Abraham Lincoln, who, as a youth, befriended a special dog. He'd found the injured animal roaming in the forest, fed her, and made a splint for her broken leg. Then he brought the dog home and named her Honey. Later, when Lincoln was accidentally trapped in a cave, where he might have died, Honey led rescuers to find him. Because of the strength of this human–animal connection, Lincoln lived to fulfill his role in history.

And, finally, Patricia Hobbs Hendry, a freelance writer from California, expresses the joy shared by angel animals and humans.

Bliss

A sigh of peace.
I have found my heaven,
My nirvana—
A cat, a crossword,
and a cup of coffee.

We hope you'll get yourself a cup of coffee, tea, or whatever you prefer, relax, and enjoy reading the next chapter. It's brimming with angel animals who teach us how to experience the greatest love of all—the kind that gives without expecting a return.

Chapter Two

Learning How to Love
Unconditionally

Never again will I settle for the phrase "only an animal" to describe one of my fellow creatures. The animals, themselves, through their loyalty, bravery, commitment, and love, have stated, more eloquently than any words might say, that we are all sentient and conscious beings, each holding within us that little spark of the divine.

—Stephanie Laland

*I*f you ask animal lovers what they like most about sharing their lives with furry and feathered friends, many of them will tell you that they appreciate the unconditional love animals give. The dog greeting you warmly no matter how tough a day you've had. The cat curling up in your lap and not caring if you're crabby. The bird perching on your shoulder to groom your hair even though it's not shaped into the latest style. Angel animals let you know that their love is here to stay.

Angel animals bring out the best in humans because they help us to reconnect with our higher natures. Angel animals reflect the love that is divine because the Divine loves unconditionally.

In "Flopsy Bun Bun Teaches About Love," Kristen Strobel of Lancaster, New York, writes about the selfless love she received from her rabbit. Kristen had to take Flopsy Bun Bun to an emergency clinic when she realized that the symptoms he was showing were far more serious than she'd previously thought. When she returned home with her beloved pet, she stayed up all night to comfort him, but began to realize that her friend was dying. Kristen writes, "He spent his last hours trying to take care of me by giving me hundreds of bunny kisses despite the fact that it was an effort because he was ill. He taught me so much about unconditional love." Kristen says that she continues to feel Flopsy Bun Bun's presence. His love has inspired her to work with animals at a local shelter where she's been able to help other rabbits.

Unconditional love keeps on giving.

The Many Facets of Love

Think of unconditional love as a diamond with many facets. The stories you're going to read in this chapter explore the love-diamond to help you recognize what needs polishing in your own life. Is learning to love yourself a good place to begin? Do you need to relax and accept love? Is it difficult for you to perform quiet acts of service without expecting thanks or praise? Are compassion, kindness, and the ability to be a good friend and listener spiritual qualities that you'd like to have more of in your life? The angel animals in this chapter demonstrate all these ways of loving and many more.

Pia, who lives in Hudiksvall, Sweden, has three children, an Islandic pony, a pig, a cat, and two dogs, both kelpies. Pia is a dog breeder and works full-time as a saleswoman. A dog named Mixa taught her how to take the first step toward having more love in her life.

How My Dog, Mixa, Crowned Me Queen of the World

PIA RONNQUIST

For many years I've been training dogs to compete in shows. I now know my profession has brought me a step forward in my personal spiritual journey.

My best dog, Mixa, was the last dog I had in competition trials. I trained her differently from her predecessors by making everything we did fun. It may have been because of these training techniques that Mixa always completely trusted me.

Mixa was the only puppy I didn't want to keep from a litter. Normally, I want to keep them all. I sold the puppies when they were eight weeks old because I already had two dogs and didn't want to raise another. But then my oldest dog became sick and I had to put him to sleep. One week after I sold all the puppies, the girl who had bought Mixa phoned and said that, sadly, she could not keep her. She commented that maybe there was a spiritual reason for Mixa's return to me. Somehow, I knew then that it was right for me to keep this dog.

When Mixa was two years old, I moved to Stockholm with my children. During this time of my life, Mixa played an important role in the spiritual path that I embarked on.

Mixa was a dog from the country, not used to being in the big city. Still, she always walked everywhere ahead of me on her leash. Her tail would be up over her back, wagging in the wind. People would try to be friendly toward her. Mixa communicated with them through her eyes. She seemed to be saying, "Do you see this? I am leading the way for the Queen of the World. She, who is the best and strongest one, lets me go before her. If you want to know something, talk to her, my Queen of the World." Walking with Mixa so proudly like this was a lovely feeling.

Mixa helped me to realize that often God wants us to lead the way. If we could trust God as Mixa trusts me, we'd never have problems. With the help of this loving dog, I learned to believe in myself. Even though I lacked self-confidence, I overcame my fears. Mixa helped me to understand more about my relationship with God and to accept that I'm a worthy person.

Mixa Recognized Truth

Mixa not only helped me to have higher self-esteem but also taught me to treat her with respect. Sometimes, I'd get very angry at Mixa if she didn't concentrate the way I wanted her to during our training sessions. I'd grab behind her ears and stare into her eyes. Then, I'd scold Mixa and tell her to stop what she was doing wrong. She'd look at me without any physical reaction, but in her eyes I could feel what she was thinking. Mixa let me know that treating her without respect isn't truth. It was as if she were saying, "My mother, the Queen of the World, does not do things like this. So this cannot be truth."

Mixa's unconditional love and ability to communicate have taught me that trusting God's love unblocks the brain by helping me become the "Queen of the World" I was always meant to be.

A Tail to Wag: Are there times when you feel a little low on the self-esteem meter? Do you need to have more unconditional love in your life by learning to love yourself? Perhaps you could imagine that you're walking down the street with Mixa leading the way. Visualize yourself holding your head high, trusting in your higher nature, and seeing the truth about yourself. You are King/Queen of the World. Mixa knows it. Why shouldn't you?

Arielle, president of The Ford Group, a public relations firm, is in partnership with her husband, Brian Hilliard, as a professional artists' manager for their company, Dharma Dreams. Arielle, who lives in La Jolla, California, had an unforgettable moment of unconditional love while swimming with the dolphins. This story is from her book, Hot Chocolate for the Mystical Soul.

A Dolphin's Love

ARIELLE FORD

It was an intensely bright summer day and I was fulfilling a life-long fantasy: swimming with dolphins! Having grown up in south Florida by the warm, soothing waters of the Atlantic, I'd long dreamed of dolphins. My favorite television show as a kid had been *Flipper*, and I'd prayed that someday I would swim side by side with dolphins and become part of their world, if just for a few moments.

Well, my dream had finally come true—and not only was I in the water with a dolphin, but she really seemed to like me. We had created our own little game. She'd roll on her back while I scratched her silken tummy with my flippers. Then she'd offer me her dorsal fin and take me on a ride around the lagoon. I lost track of time while my dolphin friend and I frolicked in the water.

I Felt Waves of Unconditional Love

At one point I found myself staring into her beautiful blue eyes and was amazed at what I saw. Not only was she looking directly at me, but I could feel waves of unconditional love radiating into me. As she continued to look at me, I realized that I'd never been loved so completely and so unconditionally as I was in that moment. It was an unforgettable moment of pure bliss. I'd always suspected that dolphins were special ambassadors on this planet, and now I knew for certain that they were ambassadors of love.

My encounter with that dolphin truly changed my life and opened my heart. I hope that someday I'll be evolved enough to look at someone and radiate love to them the way that dolphin loved me.

A Wave to Ride: Could you be a dolphin for a day? Consider trying this exercise. Look at each person or animal you meet today with the blue eyes of Arielle's dolphin—see them through the golden glow of unconditional love. Then, watch for the miracles and blessings that come as you radiate love into life around you.

Ronald is an artist and photographer from Sugar Creek, Missouri, who used to work at a large greeting card company. He has also written travel articles for a major newspaper. A special bird gave him the kind of love that can teach a lonely heart to sing again.

A Parrot Taught Me Her Song

Ronald L. Harmon

Shortly after my mother passed away, my father was diagnosed with congestive heart failure. For ten years I helped my father, and every waking moment became filled with caregiving on top of a full-time job. It was difficult for me to give so much, but love for my father motivated me to do everything I could.

After Dad died I felt alone, as if my days couldn't get any darker. Yet, I soon realized a freedom I'd never experienced during all the years of helping my father. But this was tempered by the fact that because I'd spent so much time caring for someone, my life now seemed to take on a chilling sort of emptiness.

Friends suggested that I get a pet. I thought about the idea but didn't have a clue what kind of animal best suited me. A friend from Germany visited my home after staying with a family in Canada. He kept telling me about the clever little bird his Canadian hosts had. The idea of having a bird in the house began to sound wonderful. My friend assured me that birds are clean and easy to care for. He tried hard to convince me that I should consider getting a bird companion. But a married couple I knew had a parrot. While visiting them, their parrot's loud screams made me nervous. I knew that this sort of pet wouldn't work for me. I thought about the pros and cons of dogs, cats, even guinea pigs, but I decided a bird just didn't seem to be in my future.

"I Want This Bird!"

One afternoon I went to a local shopping center and ambled into the pet store. Perched in the open near the front door sat an exquisite soft gray bird with a red tail. A couple of customers commented about how tame the little feathered creature seemed when the parrot allowed them to stroke her head. Suddenly, I found myself thinking, *I want this bird.* Immediately, though, I squelched the idea of buying a pet and left the store.

The image of the little gray bird stayed with me as my car seemed to float down the highway away from the store. Even names for the new pet drifted through my mind. After some thought, I settled on calling the bird Buddy. I'd driven about a mile or two along the highway when I decided to go back and buy Buddy no matter what the cost. That day began a relationship like none I'd ever thought could be possible with an animal.

As if in answer to my pre-Buddy loneliness, the bird liked to whistle for me when I left the room, never wanting me to be out of her sight for too long. If I didn't answer Buddy's whistle soon enough, she'd come looking for me. When friends dropped in, Buddy would climb down the ladder from the top of her cage to see who had stopped by. The minute my guests saw the little parrot she became the center of attention. My friends and I would sit on the floor and play with Buddy as she'd happily hop from one person to another lifting her foot to be picked up or performing some other trick to get our attention.

Spending Quality Time with Buddy

One of my favorite experiences with Buddy was how she re-sponded to having me read stories to her while she was still too young to talk. Some nights I read stories substituting Buddy's name for one of the characters. She seemed thrilled and listened with childlike interest. Winter nights often felt cold and dark when I got off work, but because of Buddy, my little house loomed cozy and warm. The thought of this happy little bird being there filled my heart with gratitude. In the evenings I'd sit in the television room with Buddy perched nearby on a wooden hall tree. Together we'd watch television or listen to music in comfortable companionship.

When Christmas inched closer, with my family gone, I thought it could be a really difficult and sad occasion. One comfort was that Buddy and I would be celebrating the young parrot's first Christmas together. As the cold winter mornings edged their way toward Christmas, my little friend would sit on the top of her cage and sing as if thanking God for being alive. It surprised me when some of the Christmas carols became Buddy's favorites and she'd sing along to them. Buddy in her own way added something special only she could bring to the spirit of Christmas, and I loved her for it.

Buddy was four months old when we began sharing our lives together. When I first saw the lovely African grey at the pet store, I didn't know it, but Buddy was destined to fill a void in my existence. Because of my relationship with Buddy, I no longer suffered loneliness but experienced a true expression of God's love. Buddy's companionship gives me the lasting kind of gifts that make every day Christmas.

Wings to Fly: After this story was published in the *Angel Animals* newsletter, Ronald wrote to us that he read it to Buddy. She became a little difficult to live with after attaining so much celebrity. We're sure she's recovered by now. As happened with Ronald, are you regaining hope or confidence through your relationship with an animal? One aspect of unconditional love is the willingness to listen. Is there a lonely person in your family, neighborhood, or work who would appreciate it if you listened as attentively as Buddy?

The following story is by Sri Harold Klemp, the spiritual leader of Eckankar, a religion which teaches that animals, just like people, are souls too. Harold writes extensively and has more than thirty published works to date. This story shows how two cats demonstrated the difference between jealous and unconditional love. It is from his book Unlocking the Puzzle Box.

Nubby and Sunshine

HAROLD KLEMP

At home our neighbors' beautiful black cat, Nubby, began to come over for visits just as my wife was taking our little dog outside for her daily walks. Our squeaky front door is the signal. Every time we open it, here comes the cat. Nubby visited quite a bit when she was new to the neighborhood and shy, but she kept her distance from our dog, Molly.

When my wife and Molly would go out for a walk, Nubby would come over, and pretty soon my wife began to pet the cat. My wife is basically a dog person, but somehow Nubby got to her—you know how animals can work their way into your affections. Day after day she came over to get her back scratched and petted and to hear my wife coo at her. "Nubby, you're such a pretty cat, you're so beautiful," she'd say. Though the cat never purred, her pleasure was evident in the way she would lie down and stretch out on the sidewalk, asking for more.

One day Nubby heard the door squeak open and, as usual, came hurrying over. This time she was carrying something in her mouth. She dropped the object on the lawn, nudged it toward my wife with her nose, then glanced up with a look that said, "This is for you." It was a smooth, white pebble. My wife knew that this special little treasure was Nubby's way of saying thank you. "Why, Nubby, what a beautiful gift," my wife said. "Thank you so much." Nubby, of course, just swelled up with pride.

Weeks passed, it snowed a little bit, and we forgot about the pebble. When the snow melted, we discovered that the little white pebble was still there. Nubby would come over and nuzzle it every so often, just to make sure it was okay.

Levels of Love

Nubby has a housemate named Sunshine—Sunny for short. He's a big orange cat that looks like Garfield. Because he is so hefty, his stomach sways from side to side as he waddles along the sidewalk.

Even though Sunny is very shy and standoffish, he was jealous of the fact that Nubby got all the petting. Eventually he worked up his nerve to come over and allow his fur to be stroked, but only a little bit, and then he'd run off.

One day my wife took Molly outside for a walk; I looked out the window and saw her petting Sunny. When she was finished, I happened to notice that Sunny had a very peculiar expression on his face that I couldn't quite figure out. Later I mentioned to my wife, "Sunny has started to get an odd look on his face. I wonder why."

"He's in love," she said, and I realized it was true. I hadn't thought Sunshine had any love in him at all before this, but gradually he has started to soften up. Unfortunately, his first love was based on jealousy. But even though this isn't the best kind of love, it's better than nothing.

After a while he got more competitive. As soon as our door opened, he'd race over ahead of Nubby to get petted, then turn around and shoot her a warning look: Stay back! I got here first!

And Nubby, being a sleek, dignified, feminine cat filled with pure love, knew she wouldn't stand a chance in a fight with big, muscular Sunny.

One time Nubby came tearing down the street, running as fast as she could, with Sunny hot on her heels. Suddenly she dropped flat to the ground and did a funny flip that reminded me of something I saw once when watching championship swimmers on TV. The move was so unexpected that Sunny went flying on past and couldn't stop. In the meantime, Nubby came out of the flip, ran off in the opposite direction, and made a mad dash for my wife, where she knew she'd be safe.

These two cats demonstrate the different levels of love that a soul goes through. First there is no love at all, then the soul experiences a low form of love often driven by anger, jealousy, and spite.

But as we go through different life experiences, we begin to recognize that we can't live with this sort of lower love. Gradually the jealousy goes away, and at some point we realize that the only kind of love worth anything at all is pure love. When we can see this pure love as divine love, we come to know that there is enough for everyone, for all creatures and all things.

A Paw to Lick: Are you more like Nubby, or do you see life the way Sunshine does? Do you trust that there's enough love to go around? Is there a gift you could give—your own white pebble—to someone and not expect this person or animal to belong to you in return?

Debbie is an elementary school learning disabilities teacher from Hilliard, Ohio. She loves nature, hiking, playing the piano, and writing stories for children. She lives with her daughter, Jodi, her dog, Brewster, and two cats, Puddy and Jasmin. Debbie's story reminds us that angel animals may offer us unconditional love in ways we never expected.

The Dog Who Showed Me What Love Is

DEBBIE BURKITT

A friend surprised me with the gift of a miniature pinscher dog. Although Brewster appeared healthy, it soon became obvious that he'd been abandoned and mistreated. When anyone tried to pet him, he'd duck and move away. When I called him, he'd run in the opposite direction. He'd hide under the furniture when he saw his collar and leash. But I knew there was hope for him when I noticed that he'd jump on the lap of and snuggle with anyone who sat on the couch. I could see that this dog had love in his heart. If only I knew what key would unlock it.

On the day my friend gave Brewster to me, I was feeling depressed. This little dog also seemed to be sad. He had no interest in my two cats or my friend's miniature pinscher. Brewster only wanted to snuggle and sleep with me that first night. The next morning he seemed even more sluggish. I had to carry him out of bed. The fleeting thought crossed my mind that being around me might be making Brewster more depressed than he had been. I wondered if he was empathizing with me to the point that he was relating to my sadness as if it were his own.

Later that day I silently asked God to help me understand the issue that was causing me to feel despondent. I asked for help in having a more balanced attitude about the situation. After my prayer, I felt my melancholy lifting and started feeling great. I walked around the house and found Brewster playing with my daughter and her father. They mentioned that the dog had perked up. Now my sense that perhaps Brewster was empathic became stronger.

The Happier I Got the Sadder Brewster Became

During the next few months I asked God for help with my problems and I gained many new insights. I was feeling happier and more centered than I ever remembered being. However, as my burdens were becoming lighter, Brewster seemed to be carrying a heavier load. He became lethargic, difficult to wake up in the morning, and he rarely wanted to play for more than a moment. He didn't have much energy for his daily walks. To make matters worse, Brewster wasn't housebroken and often made messes on the carpet. Friends suggested that I didn't have to keep this dog. But Brewster reminded me of my own difficult times. I thought of people who had been "angels" and helped me along the way. I decided that I wouldn't abandon Brewster, a dog who had been let down by people far too often.

I asked God to help me understand how to be a friend to a dog with a bad case of the blues. I started thinking about stories I'd heard of animals who take on some of their human friends' karma, the effects of their past actions. I suddenly realized that the problem wasn't that Brewster was empathic. Instead, he'd made my burdens his own. No wonder he was so tired!

I called Brewster and sat down to have a heart-to-heart chat with him. I thanked him for his generous act of kindness. Then I told him he didn't have to carry the load of my pain and suffering anymore.

Within a few minutes of my talk with Brewster, I began to cry and feel anger welling up inside of me. I'd been feeling fine just moments before and didn't understand what could have triggered such an emotional response. Then I remembered. I'd just told Brewster that he didn't have to help me. In some spiritual way that I can't explain, he must have given my burdens back and they felt like bricks on my chest.

Since that day when I relieved Brewster of any responsibility he might have taken for my emotional well-being, the dog blossomed. He began getting up in the morning full of energy and ready to play. He wanted to be petted. He waited with anticipation for me to put on his collar and leash and take him for walks. I started having to run to keep up with him. He played ball like a happy puppy.

I think that by letting go of my burdens, Brewster somehow realized that he could release his own past traumas. He no longer acted like an abused and abandoned animal.

It humbles me to remember that I thought I was doing Brewster a service by keeping and loving him when he was lifeless and unhappy. But God enlisted this angel animal whose unconditional love helped me to move past a difficult issue and find true joy in my life.

A Tail to Wag: Could an angel animal, with a heart full of unconditional love, be helping to carry some of your life's burdens? Is there any way you can lighten the load?

Rachel, a fourteen-year-old from Austin, Texas, says that she's been riding horses forever and that she loves horses and horse people. Her other passion is writing. Rachel's animal companion is a two-year-old golden retriever named Gus, and she adores him. She spends most of her time at the stable working as a counselor at the horse camp. In her story she tells of an angel animal who taught her how to love without expectations.

The Horse of My Dreams Is in My Dreams

RACHEL FARRIS

Sundown wasn't the horse of my dreams. To be frank, he wasn't even close. He was, however, my horse—and mine alone.

The fall I was in fifth grade, I flipped through the classified ads. I let myself begin wishing for a horse that I read about there, a "Hunter/Jumper Prospect," indicating a horse that can be trained in the English riding style of hunting and jumping, which is how I'd learned to ride. I became excited about a horse that was advertised as "Already jumping 3!"

"Christmas ponies (layaway accepted)" stood out in bold lettering and the occasional "AQHA CH Bar Nose" (American Quarter Horse Association Champion) teased me.

My eyes fell on a particular ad: "Welsh Pony, 14th Sweet. Call for details." I'd been riding horses since I was five years old, but for the last five years, whenever I'd asked my parents about purchasing one for me, they'd refused. But after reading the advertisements for horses on this day, I asked my dad about buying a horse and hinted how cute a pony would be. To my shock and joyful surprise, he said, "Wanna call them?"

I quickly nodded. This was the first time in history my dad had actually said, "Let's call them!" about a horse.

I couldn't wait to find out what this pony would be like. I imagined a well-tended stable with a riding arena and a nice instructor who would let me jump, canter, and try out the horse of my dreams. Soon enough, we were headed out in my dad's truck, with me squeezed between him and Robin, a horse-owner friend of the family who kept her horse at an expensive stable. I was currently unhappy with my instructor and stable and had high hopes that maybe owning a horse would give me the satisfaction I was looking for.

I knew it was almost impossible to think that my parents would ever be able to afford to board a horse at the stable where I rode. But I thought that maybe I could keep the pony where he currently stayed, or maybe at Robin's small barn. At this time, I simply wanted to own a horse or a pony. Anything I could ride.

We got out to the stable and my bubble burst. The mouse brown–colored bay pony, who the man had said was a "little off" in the back hind, was dead lame. The stable owner had a western saddle on him. He wasn't exactly the type of horse a girl who rides English would want. As I viewed the corral of about fifteen horses, I realized that the man must run a place where people could rent horses and go on trail rides.

I'd always wanted a palomino, and so did my dad—even though they aren't the hunter/jumper color, which is usually gray, bay, or black. But I thought palominos were beautiful. The man, who saw we were obviously disappointed in the pony, let me down. My dad asked about the rest of the horses. His eyes lit up as he pointed to the prettiest ones—a beautiful black and white paint and a well-built Morgan.

"Y'all," he said, in a rough Texan accent, "can have anyone but them two!"

Then I saw a palomino. "That one, Dad!" I said.

The man looked to the palomino. "Ah, yeah, Trigger?" He immediately began working, moving the rest of the horses into a corral.

The owner kept pointing to a furry brown horse with the letters *JD* on his shoulder, which was probably the brand for a ranch. The man had named the horse *JD*. Original, huh? He'd named the mouse-brown pony *Mouse*, and the Morgan horse was named *Morgan*.

I pushed JD aside and firmly stated that I wanted to ride Trigger. As soon as I started riding the quarter horse around the paddock, I was already thinking of names for him. When I asked Trigger to canter, he'd go about five strides and stop in front of his owner. Because of his behavior, I thought that Trigger was too loyal to this owner and would be very, very hard to train. I found out later that the horse stopped because he was so hungry and he knew that this was the man who fed him.

When we went home, I kept talking about Trigger. My mother was opposed to my getting him. He wasn't too expensive, but she thought I didn't need a horse because I could just take lessons. While we were walking around the neighborhood one evening, I kept trying to convince her that I should have a horse. All the while, I was thinking of names for Trigger. Finally, my mom said that I could get him. Since it was around sundown, I decided to call the horse Sundown Walker or Sundown for short.

Getting to Know the Horse of My Dreams

Sundown turned out to be difficult to train. He'd been working as a trail-riding horse and wasn't used to being asked to do things by the beginning riders who couldn't control him. But when I rode him, Sundown had a very smooth trot. His mane was a beautiful creamy white and his coat shone light golden. He had a flood of white hairs in a beautiful blaze going down his face. His socks were always clean with no grass stains to see. I grew to love him to bits and pieces.

When we first got Sundown as a seven-year-old, he was as

skinny as a toothpick. He'd obviously been underfed and under-nourished. But he worked up to a large bucket of sweet feed a day and slowly got back into shape.

I remember that I used to go out into the pasture while Sundown ate. I'd sit and sing to him the first song that came to mind—"Daddy's gonna buy you a mockingbird" or a new country song. I'm a terrible singer, but Sundown never minded. He'd just put his head in my hands and sort of sigh a little. I remember that I sang one song, "With a Broken Wing," because it's about someone who's been hurt and is doing well now even after being abused. There's a line in it that says, "You ought to see her fly." That song reminded me so much of Sundown. He was recovering from his previous rough life and, together, we were learning to fly.

I ended up boarding Sundown at Robin's barn. As it turned out, the barn's manager was hugely helpful. She'd hold Sundown while the farrier shod him. Sundown was deathly afraid of getting new shoes and he'd tremble and shake. But he was dearly sweet in the pasture, when he was roaming around, and even as I rode him. But he'd tense up at the sight of shoes. The only way to get him to settle was to let him nibble on sweet feed.

I also suspected that Sundown feared men, because the only man he'd let near him was my dad. I think that's because Sundown knew Dad was the one who bought him for me.

Sundown Is Flying Now

Well, Sundown and I never got to show—something I used to think was very important. We never got to jump. We never got to do flying lead changes. We never got to do so many things.

One night in March, before he turned eight years old, Sundown broke his leg while frolicking in the pasture. He had to be put down. This horse hadn't been with me for more than six or seven months, but his death hurt me so much that I stopped riding for nearly a year.

Eventually, my broken heart healed enough for me to begin

riding a seven-year-old Thoroughbred named Ricky, who is sweet and beautiful. Because Ricky is hardly trained, people ask me what I see in him. I just smile to myself as I recall the great lessons Sundown taught me. Sundown showed me what the important qualities are in a horse, or in anybody. He helped me to see that sweetness and a good heart are much more valuable than how perfectly trained or educated a creature might be. With his love, he taught me how to love unconditionally. Ricky is special in himself, but I also love him because he brings back memories of happy times with Sundown. Ricky and I ride once or twice a week. Somehow, I think Sundown would approve.

I know that Sundown is now in heaven watching over me when I ride. I take falls, but I'm never more than bruised, and the only thing broken is my pride.

Instead of being the horse *of* my dreams, Sundown has become the horse *in* my dreams, where we do things we couldn't accomplish during his life. In my dreams Sundown is never hungry or in pain. He brings back memories of our good times in the pasture, of the first time we cantered, of the day that I went to the barn and couldn't see his ribs anymore.

In my dreams Sundown and I jump; we soar. You ought to see us fly.

A Tail to Swish: Could Sundown help you view friends or family members through the eyes of unconditional love? Are there spiritual qualities you may be overlooking in people or animals because they don't measure up to all you dreamed they would be?

Prana was an angel animal dog in the Anderson family for many years. This is Linda's story of how Prana taught us about unconditional love.

What Prana, Animals, and Apples Knew About Service to Life

LINDA ANDERSON

Prana, our beautiful golden retriever whose name means "breath of life," isn't with us anymore. She died of cancer several years ago. But while sharing our home, she brought such joy and love into our lives that we still miss her. There are so many wonderful stories about the love in this dog, but my favorite is one that created an indelible image of how to graciously give what is needed without reserve.

It was an autumn day in Minnesota. But the weather didn't seem to know the difference between fall and winter. We were hit with a big snowfall for which no one was prepared.

We have two apple trees in our backyard. Prana loved apples. When she went outside, she'd grab an apple, stick it far back in her mouth, and sneak it into the house to save for nibbling on later. The apples had been on the ground and were often muddy, so I wasn't always happy that Prana had brought them into the house. Sensing my disapproval, she'd turn her head, so I wouldn't see her hidden treasure. It was our little game.

Prana Made Her Own Version of an Apple Pie

On the day that it snowed too early in the season, Prana went outside, and I watched her from the window. I noticed that she was frantically digging holes and bringing the apples to the surface so they could be seen above the snow. I wondered why she was doing this. She seemed intensely occupied with a mission to dig up as many apples as possible during her yard time.

When I called her back into the house, she carried her usual one apple in her mouth. About five minutes later, I looked outside. The yard was completely covered with birds. It looked as if Prana had dug up all those apples for her bird and squirrel friends to eat because they wouldn't have enough food to survive such an early winter! Tears sprang to my eyes as I witnessed this beautiful act of unconditional love from a creature who taught us how to serve life with such grace.

A Tail to Wag: Could you try actively looking for service you can give, like Prana's digging up the apples? Maybe you might perform acts of kindness or give love without expecting a return. Or discover the joy of doing good deeds when no one is looking. Could you fill the copy machine at work, water plants at home, cook someone's favorite dinner, or find simple ways to bring more love into your life and the lives of others?

Beverly is from Minneapolis, Minnesota. She is a writer, editor, and quilter. Married for twenty years, Beverly is the mother of two very active boys. Her family also includes Winston, a Brittany spaniel, and Lance, an Australian bearded dragon. In her story, Beverly shows how an angel animal replaced fear with love.

Lizard Love

BEVERLY FOSTER

Everything about Lance set off my defenses. Even though he was only eight inches long, his dry, bumpy skin, with little spikes down his sides, told me to beware. While the rest of the family loved our new pet, an Australian bearded dragon, I was terrified of him.

My son named him Lance and gave him a home in a glass cage. When days and then a week went by with my eleven-year-old forgetting to feed Lance, I gradually started dropping greens down to him or suppressing a gag to give him the live food his body needed.

Eventually, I was able to stroke Lance's arrow-shaped head. One day I carefully lifted him up and set him on the floor. He was terrified at first by the wide-open space, but eventually overcame his fear and began to run. I jumped back to get out of his way, afraid he might be coming to attack me.

After running back and forth a little, Lance soon had crawled up the brick hearth and found a tiny crack behind the fireplace cover. He pressed his nose into this space and breathed the draft. I left him there for his whiff of fresh air. Even though he grew stiff with cold, he seemed so happy to have this moment of freedom. I put him back in his cage to warm up. For the first time, I was beginning to understand that Lance had feelings and I could empathize.

From then on, Lance and I communicated more. Now, his actions tell me which of our visitors he likes. He's especially fond of pretty women who coo over him. His steely wariness clearly shows that he thinks of our big-pawed exuberant dog, Winston. His bright attention gives me all the thanks I need when I feed him.

When I first met Lance, he frightened me. But gradually I learned to see life from his point of view. Now, I like to hold his paws and let him dangle from my fingertips or drape him across my shoulder. I have a hard time remembering what I used to think was so scary about him. Now, he's just a quiet little friend.

A Tail to Swing: Are you turning someone—human or animal—into Godzilla when he or she is only a little lizard looking for a whiff of freedom and unconditional love? It's often said that we create our own monsters. Could Lance teach us how to face ourselves in what we fear the most and to love creatures who may be just as scared of us as we are of them?

More About Unconditional Love

Philip Gonzalez and Leonore Fleischer wrote about an angelic presence they found in a dog named Ginny. In *The Dog Who Rescues Cats*, Gonzalez reveals that he's disabled and surviving on a meager stipend. He'd been spiraling into depression and self-pity until he adopted Ginny from an animal shelter. Ginny taught Gonzalez that the way to receive is to give. She specializes in rescuing cats by leading Gonzalez to handicapped stray and abandoned cats and kittens that she finds.

It often takes courage to love unconditionally. Wayne Hudson, a composer and writer from Anstead, Australia, whose story about a koala is in chapter 7, wrote about an angel animal who brought unconditional love to his family in "Four-Paws Reminds Us to Love Each Other." Wayne says that Four-Paws the cat bravely, but gently, does whatever is necessary to remind family members to be kinder to each other if there is a conflict in the house. Once when Wayne was about to say something in the heat of an argument that he might have regretted later, the cat intervened by jumping on his lap and placing her paw on his heart. This reminded Wayne to speak out of love instead of anger. Wayne writes, "Sometimes, Four-Paws softly touches one of us with her paw. If the argument continues, she'll playfully nibble at one of the offenders. Four-Paws helps us to keep the love in our family flowing more smoothly."

The next chapter shows the many ways that we break, neglect, and form families today and how angel animals enrich and mend family life with peace, harmony, forgiveness, and patience.

Chapter Three

Creating Family Harmony

Animals are capable of great kindness and compassion; they rescue, comfort, and care for us. They are one of life's great blessings.

—Kristin Von Kreisler

*A*ngel animals are definitely important members of human families. Peter Lucchese, a publicist and media relations specialist from Goldens Bridge, New York, writes in "Pal, a Member of the Family" that his childhood dog held a special place in his home. "My mother used to tell our family to refer to Pal by his name rather than call him a dog because he might feel hurt. We had to spell certain words in front of Pal so that he wouldn't know what we were talking about. Every Halloween we'd dress up Pal in his own costume. For 'Brother Pal's' birthday, Mom would bake a cake and Pal sat at the kitchen table in his own chair to celebrate."

We can find angel animal families outdoors as well as in our houses. Patricia Fish, an avid bird lover and author from Pasadena, Maryland, learns about parenting from birds in her backyard, which she's named Critter Cove. In "Bird Children," Patricia writes, "For two months I will be entertained by the sight of harassed parent birds and awkward offspring. I will watch them learn to take a bath, find their own worms, and store food. By the time of winter's fury, the adolescents will be ready to join the flocks, fully trained and healthy to survive the elements. My own child stands tall, proud, and healthy. We all, birds and humans, must go through it. I think our smiles spring from the wonderful sight of our species' continuation."

Loving Our Families Is a Spiritual Gift

Angel animals help us see firsthand in a family the power of love to overcome any obstacle. Kristy Walker, a nutritional researcher from Austin, Texas, writes in her story "Misha, the Good Daddy Cat" that her two Siamese cats, Misha and Bani, were new parents to three beautiful babies. Kristy had heard that it's important not to leave a male cat with kittens, so she carefully separated Misha from Bani and their kittens. While Kristy's niece visited and spent time in the bedroom with the cloistered new mother and her babies, she heard Misha, then saw his paw shoving kitty toys under the door. After this Kristy says, "I let Misha also be responsible for the children. Misha would pick up the kittens and help Bani move them. He'd lick them clean and when Bani took a break from mothering, Dad took over by curling up to sleep with his babies. What an example of a father!"

The stories you're about to read in this chapter show angel animals forming, enriching, and healing families in the most amazing and instructive ways.

Enjoy!

Deborah is from Colorado Springs, Colorado. She worked for many years as a United States Air Force attorney and was assigned to the chief prosecutor's position while stationed in Europe. She loves animals and has dreams of creating an animal shelter to give a permanent home to large animals no one else wants. In this story, Deborah shares how her cat helped her adjust to becoming a full-time mom to her daughter.

How a Cat Helped Me Cope with First-Time Parenthood

DEBORAH WOLUSKY

I first saw Aiko at an animal shelter in the spring of 1993 when she was a four-week-old stray female cat. After I brought her home, my husband and I got a book for naming babies. When we found *Aiko*, which in Japanese means *little beloved*, we knew this would be the perfect name for her.

Aiko is a beautiful black and white shorthaired cat. She's slightly plump because she'll eat about anything. She's slept in our bed ever since she was a kitten.

About a year and a half after we adopted Aiko, our daughter was born. It had been a difficult birth. My husband and I were completely inexperienced and we had no one to help us. Suffering from a terrible case of the "baby blues" and feeling highly stressed, I cried on and off all day long. To make matters worse, the baby didn't sleep more than ten hours out of twenty-four and when she did, it was only for short periods. While awake, the baby had to be held as I walked around the room or bounced her on my lap. If I even tried to relieve the tension by reading a book while holding her, she'd cry. I had to focus completely on the baby, sometimes for hours, often in the middle of the night when I was dead tired.

The Baby's Cries Upset Aiko

When I brought the baby home, Aiko was frightened by her crying. She'd run from the room at the first sound of distress. Even when the baby was quiet, Aiko acted nervous and upset around her. Despite her uneasiness, Aiko always stayed nearby. Instead of sleeping upstairs in her cozy bed, when I was awake all night rocking the baby, Aiko curled up next to me. Wherever I went in the house, day or night, Aiko stayed with me. Her presence brought unbelievable comfort to a new, insecure mother.

I didn't realize what a toll Aiko's vigilance took until she began to cough and wheeze. Our veterinarian said that Aiko had asthma. Since she'd never been sick, the vet asked a lot of questions about what had changed in Aiko's environment and said that the stress of a new baby could have made Aiko sick.

The medication the vet prescribed didn't work, and Aiko degenerated over the weekend. Her wheezing attacks were horrible to watch; she was having trouble breathing. Despite her weakened body and worsening sickness, Aiko still sat with me during all those long hours with the baby in the middle of the night. I took Aiko, who now was literally turning blue from lack of oxygen, back to the vet, where she was given injections. Aiko came very close to dying, but the injections worked. In a couple of weeks Aiko was cured and she hasn't been sick again.

Aiko Never Left My Side

Even though my cat was so ill that she could have died, Aiko stayed by my side near the baby. This must have been the last place on earth she wanted to be. I love our *little beloved* with all my heart and she certainly has shown her love for me.

Now that my daughter is eighteen months old, Aiko will let

the toddler touch and even hug her. I'm sure this isn't her favorite thing to have happen because my daughter pulls Aiko's tail. When my daughter is older, I look forward to telling her how much Aiko helped me to take care of her when she was a little baby. If Aiko could talk, I'm sure she would agree it was a grueling but rewarding experience.

> **A Paw to Lick:** Is there a child in your life now, or one you could befriend, who needs the kind of attention and support Aiko gave? Perhaps you know a youngster who is going through a tough time—and making life rough for others—today, but whose future and well-being is worth your effort. Could Aiko's courage and love inspire you to go the extra mile?

Kellie, a stay-at-home mother, artist, and writer from Irving, Texas, enjoys gardening, pets, raising her two sons, and volunteering for her church. She currently shares her home with animal companions China, a chow/lab mix; Shake, a Quaker parrot; Kioki, a cat; a black kitten named Nala; two rabbits, Phillip and Cocoa Puff; and many fish. In this story, Kellie shares two essential spiritual qualities for having better family relationships.

Two Birds Taught Remorse and Forgiveness

KELLIE SISSON SNIDER

Our family adopted a budgie we named Max. I tried to teach Max to talk and spent lots of one-on-one time with him when the family was away during the day, but finally had to conclude that Max would be a sweet nontalker. Despite our attentions, Max was quiet until we adoped a Quaker parrot named Shake. Max didn't speak until Shake began to do so, but in no time, he could duplicate Shake's large vocabulary. While Shake spoke to everyone, Max spoke only to Shake.

As I watched the two birds, it became apparent that Max had become intrigued by Shake's ability to speak English. He imitated Shake's every word and wanted to be right in front of him to observe his beak, dance around, or talk to Shake all the time. Max wouldn't leave Shake alone, whether the birds were in or out of their cages. Max's obsessive need to be near his friend was driving Shake nutty.

One day, while I was out of the room, Shake was climbing inside of his cage. Max was walking around Shake's cage pestering him, as usual. I rushed back when I heard Max's desperate screams. Shake, his frustration building over Max's constant attention, had reached through the bars and bitten the toe of his buddy who loved too much. The horrible wound revealed Max's flesh was open to the bone and his toe was broken. Max's toe had to be amputated and the bird was in terrible pain for several days.

Shake Thought About What He'd Done

While Max recovered, a strange thing started to happen. I'd moved Shake's cage across the room to protect Max. But the injured bird began calling, "Shake! Shake!" And Shake would answer by calling back, "Max! Come here, Max! Come on!" Their mournful cries were sad to hear, but I couldn't risk having Max get hurt again, so I kept the birds separated.

When Max had healed, I got a female budgie, Angel. I hoped the new bird would bond with Max and help him recover from losing Shake's companionship.

Then I noticed something new in Shake's behavior. A couple of days after the accident, Shake began to spend a long time "beaking" his toes. He knew what toes were because I played a game of "I'm going to get your toesies!" with him every day. But on this day, Shake examined his toes thoroughly, going over them while mumbling something. It took a while for me to understand what he was saying, until he finally talked louder.

He was whining, in a very sad voice, "Ma-a-ax. Oh, Max. Ow, Max. Ow, toesies. Ma-a-ax. Ma-a-ax." It seemed as if Shake were realizing what he'd done to his friend. In his own way, he was saying that he was sorry.

Max Fell in Love

Six weeks after Max and Shake were separated, Max indeed began to fall in love with Angel. I was able to move Shake's cage back beside the couple, but I left plenty of space in between the two cages so that no beaks could reach birds' toes. I also closely supervised any times the birds spent outside of their cages. Now, a much happier and safer Max spends his days expressing his love for the more receptive Angel.

But Shake still cries out to Max. Although Shake can imitate words by listening to us talk, he strings them together to express his regret as he plaintively calls, "Max, Max. Come 'ere! Where's your toesies?"

I feel that from these two birds I've learned a valuable lesson about having compassion. And I saw, firsthand, that animals show remorse and are willing to forgive.

Wings to Fly: Could you, like Max, find it in your heart to forgive someone in your family who has hurt you? Shake's ability to express how sorry he was for injuring Max shows us how angel animals mend their family rifts. Would you want to do the same?

Sally is from Hartland, Wisconsin. She works as a corporate controller and systems administrator. Sally has lived in her neighborhood for fifteen years and belongs to a civic group that works within this community to make it a better place by donating money to charitable organizations. She enjoys computers, crafts, and, of course, animals. Sally shares a remarkable story of three angel animal dogs who formed a family circle that has protected and comforted her.

The Family of Miracle Workers

SALLY A. VOELSKE

I've been blessed to have a family of three wonderful dogs who have taught me many spiritual lessons and helped me through some of my toughest times. Before my husband and I were married, we adopted a little Maltese puppy we named Puff and a large golden retriever named Rusty. I'd grown up with the idea that nobody wants to listen to me talk about my problems, so I reveal them to only a select few. These dogs became my private listening club. I could release my problems by talking things out with them. Unlike some people, they gave me no judgmental feedback.

I developed a seizure disorder brought on by too much stress. When Rusty was around me at home, he could be in the farthermost corner of the house, but five minutes before I was to have a seizure, he would come to my side to warn me. I know it wasn't a coincidence because he did this every time.

When I woke up from the seizure, Puff would be lying close to comfort me. I believe Puff and Rusty knew I was scared and needed their help.

The Special Bond Between Rusty and Me

From day one, Rusty and I had an unbelievable bond between us. He was always there helping me through everyday turmoil. I can understand why golden retrievers work well as dogs for the handicapped. They're bright and intuitive. They seem to know what to do even before a need is expressed.

At the age of thirteen years, Rusty passed on before his sister, Puff. I was with him when he had to be put to sleep. He was always there for me and I couldn't and wouldn't leave him in his final hour. He fell asleep in my arms. This was one of the hardest days in my life. For months, I was horribly upset. Puff was lost without her buddy, so I grieved for her as well. I buried my emotions deep inside of me because I didn't want to be thought of as an emotional female.

And my seizures still happened.

Puff did all she could to comfort me and I tried to console her. During this sad time, I kept hearing Rusty's nails clicking on the linoleum floor. I heard him groan as he used to do when rolling over. My grief was so great. I felt people would think I was strange, so I tried to keep a happy exterior. Puff became my only confidante.

One night, six months from the day Rusty left us, after I'd had a hard time falling asleep, he came to me in a dream. With his eyes bright and tail wagging, Rusty nuzzled my ear as he'd done so many times when he was alive. After that dream, I awoke with a totally different attitude. I knew Rusty was okay and happy to be free of his arthritis and old-age pains.

Puff II Completed My Family's Circle

Puff stayed with us for another five years. Finally, old age took her when she was eighteen. Since Puff was our last dog, my husband and I decided that we'd go petless, but after a year I needed a new, uncritical friend who I could talk to.

One day, my husband surprised me by bringing home a quarter-pound Maltese puppy. We named her Puff II. She was small, sickly, and needed twenty-four-hour care. She went to work with me and slept behind my desk in a plastic bucket. Every two to three hours, she'd wake up and squeak. I'd warm baby food and spoon-feed her. My feelings of self-worth returned because I again had a friend and a creature to mother.

My little dog was the smallest of the litter, and her body didn't produce sugar properly for the first year. She'd go into sugar shock and have seizures, just as I did. The fact that we both had seizures made me feel as if we'd been brought together to help each other through this devastating disorder. During the period when Puff II had seizures, I cared for her around the clock. I greatly appreciated that the company I worked for allowed me to bring my dog to work with me. The bonds of love, compassion, and understanding between us grew incredibly strong.

Puff II Returned the Gift

Puff II is now a healthy dog. Although I am better able to manage my seizures, Puff II cuddles into my side, just as her predecessor, Puff I, did, reassuring me as if she understands. Her vigilance demonstrates the spiritual principle that what goes around, comes around.

Puff II has taught me not to be so serious and to realize that life is only a temporary reservation on this planet. She's helped me to enjoy the simple things. She's there when I need ears to listen that don't scrutinize what I'm saying. She has the heart of a great Dane and a gusto for living. She's shown me how to leap over problems and leave them behind me.

Some people look at me with concern when I express how my dogs have helped me. But I believe that everything and everyone is on this earth to teach me something. My little guardian angel, Puff II, is currently teaching me much.

> **A Tail to Wag:** Is it possible that Puff II's seizures prepared her to be Sally's guardian angel during her seizures? Will your ills today form a circle of compassion for other family members tomorrow?

Michael works to rehabilitate orphaned and injured wildlife in Valrico, Florida. He shares how a family of raccoons adopted him as one of their own.

The Raccoons Adopted Me

MICHAEL ABBOTT

In 1992 I started taking a light interest in raccoons. I didn't think much about it at the time, but now I realize that my relationship with raccoons changed my life.

I began to read about raccoons, but I noticed that there wasn't much information. So, I decided to find some raccoons and learn more about them for myself. I discovered a great place to study and, for even more fun, photograph them. I began to notice that each raccoon had a unique appearance, and they were all individuals.

The best part, though, was that the raccoons began to notice and could distinguish me from other humans. When that happened, they became easier to photograph. As the days passed, I found their interest in me growing. They'd go about their business, passing by me without concern. They'd even directly approach me a number of times so one or the other of them could take a closer look. Then I started bringing food along with me when I visited and enjoyed the pleasure of eating in the woods. Sharing food became a big hit. Before long, some raccoons would allow me to pet them; a few loved it, but others didn't want to be touched.

Special Relationships with Darknose, Harry, and Ridge

I named all my regular raccoon friends. Darknose, a yearling male who was still a virgin, became my great friend. He loved to be groomed. When I petted and rubbed him, he showed obvious pleasure. His best friend and traveling buddy, Harry, also liked to be touched.

When I groomed Darknose, he'd lie back and spread his legs as I groomed him from his chin to his rump. When he wanted me to groom a certain area, he'd gently place his little hands on mine and guide me to it. We also slept together on the forest floor.

After a while the raccoons became my friends. I went for walks with Darknose a few times. Born and raised wild, he could have scampered off, but he chose to walk by my side through the forest. We greatly enjoyed each other's company.

Another raccoon, Ridge, liked to use my lap as a warm place to nap. All the regulars, even the ones who declined to be petted, trusted me enough to leave their treasured little cubs with me for an hour or so. I felt honored that these wild animals asked me to baby-sit their young. They even allowed me to view their mating rituals at close range—a very lively activity. And they weren't at all shy.

So, that's how I got to know raccoons for what they really are!

A Tail to Thump: Although Michael was very careful while doing his firsthand research with raccoons, people who study animal behavior don't recommend approaching raccoons in the wild.

Using Michael's open-minded approach, would you like to deepen and strengthen relationships in your own family? If you want a closer relationship with someone—animal or human— check things out for yourself. Tread gently. Approach with respect. Build trusting relationships slowly and carefully. And, be the first to give.

Carol is a real estate agent and writer from Columbus, Ohio, who is working on a book about "Finding Mr. Right." Carol says that one of the best parts of her job is meeting hundreds of pets every year as she takes potential buyers into homes. This story shows how angel animals come in many shapes and forms.

A Family with Fluffy Love

CAROL FRYSINGER

I've been going through a cycle in my life where I'm attempting to find romantic love, the kind that is fluffy, warm, and sometimes seems unattainable. I'm at an age where many people are settled into relationships. It's been hard for me to break through my fears of loving someone again. No longer in a youthful body (although not bad for decades of wear and tear), I sometimes battle feelings of inadequacy and hopelessness. One day I had the charming experience of learning a powerful lesson about how families come together and relationships form. It made me realize that, regardless of the body you're in, or the role you play within a relationship, it's what's in a person's heart that matters most of all.

One day I mistakenly brought a prospective buyer to the door of a home with a "for sale" sign in the yard. Right street, wrong house. I hadn't made an appointment to show this property. But the owner graciously invited us in anyway.

Two similar-looking little girls and a boy greeted us in the living room. The ages of these children were probably three, five, and seven, and they were absolutely adorable.

The youngest girl was petting what I thought was a gray and white guinea pig or hamster named Fluffy. I noticed that this animal looked at me with absolute tranquillity, and I saw an amazing gaze of love in his eyes. The little girl passed Fluffy to her sister, who began to turn him upside down, swing him around, pet him hard, and toss him gently from hand to hand. Fluffy never resisted or protested but remained incredibly calm and relaxed.

Then I saw his long, hairless tail.

A Rat for a Pet?

"Is that a rat?" I asked, not hiding my shock very well.

"Yes," the father said. "And, he's a vegetarian."

"Doesn't he have big teeth?" I asked.

"He has some small teeth, but he never claws or bites," he answered patiently. I could tell this man had been through explanations often and had found the most effective responses.

While we visited, the three children kept passing Fluffy around, petting him overzealously. Again, I was in awe because it looked as if the little rat were smiling at me with absolute serenity and peace on his face. I couldn't believe Fluffy didn't mind the children's constant handling.

"I've never seen any pet put up with so much!" I said.

"He loves it," the father said.

"Is he a special breed?" (*This can't really be a rat,* I'm still thinking.)

"No, just a domestic rat, I guess. We got him at the pet store. My wife is allergic to cats and dogs, but Fluffy doesn't bother her."

I marveled at how this soul, who might have come to the world in a cat or dog body, had joined this family as a rodent. He'd obviously found and was fulfilling his spiritual purpose by serving as the family's guardian angel and trusted playmate.

That day, I went on with the business of selling homes, but there was an extra spark of gratitude in my heart. For I'd been blessed with the uplifting experience of encountering a special creature. Fluffy showed me that your body has nothing to do with your capacity to give and receive love. By meeting this family, I was reminded that when the right loving heart comes into my life for romance, even if I'm having a bad-hair day, that someone special will recognize the love that I have to give. Just as I'd been touched by the unconditional love flowing through Fluffy's golden heart and shining in his calm eyes.

An Idea to Consider: Could an angel animal help to form a family of loving individuals? Do angel animals help us find and recognize love in its many manifestations—even when it enters our hearts as "fluffy" romance?

Janice is a published writer. At her home in Pittsburgh, Pennsylvania, she teaches piano, guitar, violin, and Kodaly Solpage, which involves learning music through the child's own musical instrument, the voice. Janice's story shows an angel animal who used his tenacity and persistence, two important spiritual qualities, to achieve a goal.

How Joe, the Cat, Got a Couch of His Own

Janice M. Waddleton

In most families, individuals don't all have the same goals. I wanted a beautiful, loving home with attractive furnishings. Joe had a major desire in his life. He yearned to have a couch of his own. So, he had to train a family of humans to fulfill his wish.

When I adopted Joe as a kitten, he chose me to be his faithful friend. I chose him because he made me smile. He had short, thick gray fur with black stripes; one made a beautiful necklace around his proud and high chest. His underbelly was an unusual cream color. The most extraordinary thing about Joe, apart from his mammoth ears, was the beauty of his penetrating eyes, which didn't waver or deviate when he looked at someone.

When I met Joe, he was destined to go to an animal shelter along with his sister. They were the last of a litter that hadn't yet found homes. I had no intention of getting a cat. Silently, Joe followed me with those riveting eyes as I helped my friend with moving boxes. Soon, I felt compelled to look at him closely. I saw a calm, confident, charming, and funny creature. I picked him up, holding him over my head. He purred. I put him down. He returned to his sitting position. I put my finger out, to see if he'd follow it. As it came closer to his nose, he stared persistently at my finger until his eyes crossed. I took this funny and regal-looking creature home for my son and me.

Joe was to grow into one of the most exotic cats I've ever seen. He'd lie with his long limbs stretched out in front of him, looking like a sphinx. When I picked him up, he'd wrap his front legs, like a child's arms, around my neck.

Joe Liked to Scratch

Joe pleased in all ways except one. He liked to scratch. Now, all cats scratch, but he chose a gift from a friend, my new couch, to become his personal scratching post. Joe became engaged and married to his new couch habit. I went to the beach and dragged home a big log to distract him. He sat on the log, contemplating his next attack on the sofa. I should have trained him. Instead, he figured out how to train me.

Soon, big holes appeared on both arms of the couch. When the friend who had given me the couch came over, I covered the arms with two blankets and tried to pass it off as art. I think she was suspicious.

One day, I saw Joe walk into the arm of the couch. I cringed. His new sleeping place was now *inside* the sofa, and he'd conveniently torn an entryway. When the couch was unfolded to become a bed, Joe wouldn't budge from it.

My Fiancé Had to Be Trained

When I met my future husband, Phil, he was astounded by the damage to my couch. To help blend our new family and make Phil feel comfortable, I agreed to let him train Joe. "After all," he said, "I've trained horses and I can train a cat." A very disciplined guy, Phil had been a fighter pilot in the Canadian Air

Force for years. Whenever Joe scratched the couch, Phil removed him while Joe looked at me with a glint in his eye.

Phil spent months training Joe. The cat never scratched the couch when we were around, but he carried on, unabated, when we were out. We finally concluded that it had been Joe who trained Phil to relinquish the couch. When we moved, we didn't try to take the pathetic-looking thing with us and gave it away.

We bought a house, but didn't want to buy an expensive couch that could suffer the same fate as the previous one, so we purchased a small, inexpensive sofa. Joe destroyed this couch too. We tried to hide the holes, but Phil cringed when we had visitors. He'd say, "Joe runs the show."

Finally, we couldn't stand it any longer. We bought two lovely couches. During the day, we covered them with plastic and uncovered them in the evening when we used the living room.

Joe didn't scratch the couch anymore, but by the time he was fifteen years old, apart from looking a little ragged, he was as handsome as ever and very active. Then, Joe became ill. I took him to the vet. At first, they couldn't diagnose the problem. Then they realized that his spleen was enlarged. They did an ultrasound test and discovered a mass of cancer cells on his liver and spleen and in his bloodstream. It was most unusual—the kind of cancer that dogs get. We always thought that Joe had doglike qualities because he wasn't afraid of anybody and liked lots of attention.

After Joe died, we missed him, and still do, as a treasured member of our family.

I'm a music teacher and give lessons in my home. My students loved and admired Joe for years. A few days after Joe's parting, one of my students, knowing the cat had been ill, came in for a lesson and said, "I think that Joe died."

I said, "He did." Then I asked her how she knew.

She said, "Because the couches are uncovered."

> **A Paw to Lick:** Not everyone in a family has the same goals and dreams. Are there people or animals in your family who may need your patience as they attempt to achieve goals in life that you don't share? Perhaps you have a goal and Joe could inspire you to keep on scratching until you achieve it.

More Family Harmony

In Sue Cassidy's story, "Pepper, a Family Dog," an angel animal shows the way to family harmony. Sue, a writer and photographer from Huntington Beach, California, writes, "When my little boy giggles at Pepper pulling his sock off and running away with it, I've learned to laugh over the little things. When my teenage daughter sleeps beside Pepper, holding the puppy like a teddy bear, I've learned not to judge that little-girl book by its grown-up-looking cover. When my husband, who eats roofing nails for breakfast and oozes testosterone, hunkers over little Pepper, cooing softly and rubbing her belly, I've learned that men are much more gentle and nurturing than we women give them credit for. From a puppy, I've learned so much in such a short time."

Angel animals even parent us when we need it. In "Ninja Makes Sure I Eat Breakfast," Teri Olcott, a graphic artist and sports photographer from Montrose, Pennsylvania, writes about some mothering she received from her dog, Ninja. One cold winter day, Teri was shoveling out from under a foot of snow and ice. Late for work, she was getting hot, tired, and hungry. Three times Ninja sat on Teri's feet so she'd stop working so hard. Later, Ninja returned with something in her mouth. Teri writes, "I stopped shoveling, exhausted, and watched as Ninja dropped a mouthful of dog food at my feet. Knowing that Ninja, who usually devoured all her food immediately, must have saved some for me that day, I gave the dog a big hug."

In the next chapter, you'll meet angel animals who can encourage you to find a higher purpose in your life by learning what it is that you have to give.

Chapter Four

Being Inspired to Pursue a Greater Good

If we open our hearts to other creatures and allow ourselves to sympathize with their joys and struggles, we find they have the power to touch and transform us. There is an inwardness in other creatures that awakens what is innermost in ourselves.

—Gary Kowalski

*A*ngel animals teach us by their example how to work for a greater good. With their ability and willingness to serve and give, they demonstrate the spiritual qualities that inspire us to become better human beings than we ever thought we could be.

In "Puss Puss Teaches How to Be an Angel," Glenna Moore, a nurse from Hawaii, writes about an applehead Siamese cat she and her husband, Harry, adopted from a local humane society. Each night Puss Puss sleeps on top of her husband's head and saves his life. Harry has sleep apnea, which means he stops breathing while sleeping; this condition kills thousands each year. Instead of buying an expensive machine to awaken him, Harry has relied on Puss Puss for thirteen years. When Harry isn't breathing, the cat paws his face, stimulating him to breathe again; then the cat resumes purring to let Glenna know that her husband is all right. Glenna writes, "Puss Puss is a loving and devoted friend and guardian angel to us."

What if we aspired to the greater good and cared for each

other with the vigilance and love Puss Puss has shown toward Harry and Glenna for so many years?

And how often have we heard of people who ignore cries for help from a stranger, or even a neighbor? Perhaps an angel animal could show us how to respond to a greater calling and help someone who needs us.

In "Bishop Answers a Call for Help," Lynn Duffey, resource director from Las Cruces, New Mexico, writes about an experience that impressed her. "When I was recovering from gall bladder surgery, my cat, Bishop, was certainly an angel for me!" Lynn says that she was sleeping on an old couch in her mother's house and couldn't climb upstairs to use the bathroom. She accidentally rolled off the couch and fell on the floor. Lynn called for help, but her mother was sleeping upstairs and couldn't hear her. Bishop, sitting at the bottom of the steps, ran upstairs, cried loudly until Lynn's mother woke up, followed her downstairs, and made sure that Lynn received help.

Allen's Inspiration

When Allen did police work in Atlanta's inner city, he often answered calls from people whose arguments had escalated into violent confrontations. It was never a pretty sight to find couples who were arguing and hurting each other physically, especially when they were doing this in front of their children.

One night Allen answered a dispatch at a home where the couple was so busy doing violence to each other that they had completely forgotten their eight-year-old boy, who sat trembling on the sofa. While Allen calmed the situation, he glanced over to see if the child was all right. To his relief, he saw that the family's dog had jumped on the couch with the little boy and was comforting the youngster by licking his tears.

In that moment, Allen knew that someday he wanted to bring to people's attention the angelic scenes like this that he'd witnessed in police work. So often it was an angel animal who showed compassion, wisdom, and maturity while the humans acted just the opposite. He feels that the seeds for launching our project of raising awareness of animals as precious gifts through storytelling were planted in him that night as he watched with gratitude when a dog brought peace and comfort to a distressed child.

The stories in this chapter illustrate angel animals, with their many spiritual qualities, helping humans to aspire to live their lives with giving, serving, and loving as the cornerstones.

Harry lives in Portland, Oregon. He's volunteered in Search and Rescue (SAR) programs since 1972 and started training dogs for this type of work in 1986. By 1998 he and his dogs completed 370 search missions and located 263 people. Harry shares some incredible examples of his working partner, Ranger, as told to him by the dog.

My Work with the Search and Rescue Man

RANGER OAKES AS TOLD TO HARRY E. OAKES JR.

I started in Search and Rescue (SAR) when my handler, Harry, came to the dog pound and saved me from certain death. I was four months old at the time. I thought the life of a search dog would be easy. Just sit by the fireplace with a keg of brandy underneath my collar, then go play in the snow.

Was I wrong!

First, I had to learn how to read sign and body language, whistle commands, and keep up with Harry's mood swings. I had to know how to sit, stay, heel, come, get down in motion, and speak on command. Then I needed to master climbing ladders to reach trapped victims, rappel down cliffs, and swim in white water. Oh, yes, and get in and out of small spaces.

The most important skills I had to acquire were to track and air-scent by developing my ability to smell. As humans or animals walk, they shed about one thousand cells per day. I know how to smell where they've been and which way they've traveled. If it's raining hard, the rain washes the scent down, but I can still smell it. When a person stays in one place, the wind and air currents strike into them and I can pick up the scent when it's carried downwind. Heat can dry up the scent. That's why I like to search at night, because the scent stays low to the ground and it's usually cooler, so my sinus passages don't dry out.

I have so many more scent-receptor cells than humans do that I can smell hundreds of times better than them. This makes me highly qualified to help locate missing persons, if I do say so myself. When people smoke around me, though, it can numb my nose and make me useless for tracking for up to eight hours. That's why none of the dog handlers in our unit smoke.

When I'm trying to find one person among many, I need what is called a scent article. This is usually something that belongs to the missing person and hasn't been exposed to cigarette smoke or handled by anyone else. A shoe or dirty sock works real well. Harry places the scent article into a paper sack and introduces it to me. Then I check out all the smells in the area. If the scene hasn't been contaminated too badly, I track and eventually find the missing person. I've followed uncontaminated scents that were up to three months old. Usually, to be successful, I should start tracking within twenty-four hours from the PLS—that's rescue talk for "point last seen."

How I Find You If You're Lost or Injured

I'm taught to search two different ways. The first is called a general rule-out search or area search. Harry tells me to find everyone in an area and show him where they are. We use this technique if we're searching at night for plane crash, disaster, or avalanche victims. Harry may not know how many are buried under the rubble, so it's my job to find people and tell him where they are and if they're alive.

The second way of searching is more specific. When a human is buried under debris, water, snow, mud, or dirt, the scent evaporates to the surface and pools there. If the person is alive, I can smell this and it makes me so happy that I bark, wag my tail, and try to dig him out immediately. Harry gets the message and pulls me away. He then helps to dig out survivors. If people are dead, they give off a different scent. When I smell this one, I get really upset. My tail goes between my legs and I paw at the surface very slowly. Harry marks the location and moves on to the next search area.

I'm trained to find as many live victims as possible. After the area is cleared of living people, then we have the grim job of locating and removing the dead. Sometimes I'm overwhelmed with sadness and I know how upset my handler feels. We sit, hug each other, and try to make sense of what we're seeing.

One of My Most Memorable Experiences

In 1990, a call came in one day from the Seattle/King County Disaster Team to tell us that they needed four dog teams to respond with them to the earthquake in the Philippines. People from all walks of life—doctors, nurses, firemen, paramedics, and structural engineers—went with us on the free Continental Airlines twenty-hour ride to the earthquake site.

After we arrived, we were trucked to a military base where we were loaded onto helicopters to fly into the jungles and mountains. It was very hot and humid. I could see that Harry was a bit concerned as we flew over rice paddies and huts. This terrain brought memories of his days in the army in Vietnam.

We landed on a hillside that was barely still there. Mud and rock slides were everywhere. We saw a place where lots of buses and cars were buried. Harry put me to work at this site. As I searched, I could smell humans under the mud and rock. I had to give Harry the death alert and I could see hope fade from his eyes. We moved on and found out later that at this spot, the army uncovered fifty-five dead bodies. No survivors.

During the next six days, we worked around the clock, searching for victims and treating the sick and injured. It was difficult to search when I could smell death all around me. In fact, Harry had some of the nurses hide for me so I could find live victims to cheer me up because I was getting depressed.

Harry was quiet. He kept me close. I could see the pain and suffering were getting to him. I heard him say that this scene reminded him of his experiences in the service. I could often hear Harry praying at night for the strength and guidance to keep going. God was listening and helped all of our team pull through this nightmare. We found 59 dead people buried in the rubble and helped to treat 289 injured.

The death toll went up to sixteen hundred people with thousands of others left injured and homeless. We did the best we could, working through fourteen aftershocks, rock and mud slides, heat, snakes, insects, and disease.

The day before we left, we visited the Filipino Palace and met with the woman who was president then, Corazon Aquino. She thanked all of us dogs and rescuers for our efforts to help the people. Harry and the rescuers were given coffee cups. We dogs were the first to ever be allowed into the Filipino Palace. We knew that in the Philippines, it's a different culture and they view us dogs, especially ones in the jungle, as potential food. So, we watched our tails at all times.

It took Harry quite a while to readjust to the routine at home. Both of us spent a lot of quality time with each other and Brandon, Harry's son. An experience like this makes a person, or dog, stop and think. You realize how fragile, yet precious, this existence is. It makes us work even harder to save lives.

My Time on Earth Was Finished

By the time I left this work, and earth, I'd traveled more than 250,000 miles and put in over 200,000 hours in training, testing, and search missions. I performed my missions in twenty-six states and six countries. I'd found 157 victims on 370 searches and had become one of the top SAR dogs in the world. I also helped Harry go to schools and organizations to tell people how to increase their chance of being found if they were ever in an accident or lost in the wilderness. I was given hundreds of awards for my efforts and was the first SAR dog to win a position in the Oregon Pet Hall of Fame. You might find it interesting to know that I also was the first dog to win the National Association for SAR Swift Water Award because I jumped into the Pacific Ocean and risked my life to help Harry pull two drowning children from the cold waters.

When I went over to the other side, Harry said, "I lost my best friend, my partner. The world lost a true hero."

A Tail to Wag: Ranger inspires with the enormity of his dedication and service to life. As you think about this story, are there elements of Ranger's volunteer spirit that encourage you to find out how to help people and animals who have been hurt or injured?

*Bo lives with her husband, two small children, a couple of hamsters,
and a half-dozen fish in Massillon, Ohio. She publishes* The Shifting
Times, *a local metaphysical newspaper. By watching a spider, Bo
learned some important spiritual lessons about persistence and patience
that helped in her work.*

Henry, the Spider, Wove a Web of Creativity for Me

Bo Wise

The summer that Henry came to stay at my house was pregnant
with potential. I'd hatched several long-term projects and was
bringing them to fruition. Everything seemed to be falling into
place. It was as if I were about to catch a plane or train and all I
had to do was to show up. It was effortless.

Henry was a spider who had built a web in my picture window.
I decided to look up the word *spider* in my animal books. Accord-
ing to lore, the spider is mythologically responsible for having
brought about the written word. "Spider" is supposed to have created the primordial alphabet that replaced petroglyphs. Ancient
symbols can be seen in the angles of a spider's web. I also read
that the spider had helped to weave the dream of creation.

Reading about the spiritual purpose of the spider caused me to
start connecting this current phase of my life with Henry's presence. It was as if we were somehow working together. My projects had to do with spreading and recording the word. Henry's
appearance confirmed for me that I was on the right track. I believed that it was no coincidence Henry came into my life when
I'd entered a highly creative period. By the end of the summer,

this spider had helped me to become more successful in achieving my goals.

Henry and I Designed a Working Schedule

Watching that spider was like being a child and having an ant farm again. Every morning I drew the drapes and said hello to Henry, who would almost certainly be snuggled up in the corner under his silk lean-to. I'd examine his web to see if he'd repaired it during the night. I began to notice that he fixed it up about every three days.

Everyone in the neighborhood thought I was crazy to let a spider, and a fairly large one at that, hang out on the front of our house. But they came to know that no one had better harm one strand of Henry's web. He was a real hit with the kids, and I was comic relief for everyone else as I told stories about Henry's exploits and what I was learning from him.

It was always interesting to watch Henry nimbly spin prey with his front legs while wrapping it with his two back legs using the sticky substance that came from the silk ducts in the back of his body. I read that a one-inch rope of spider silk can hold up to seventy tons and is three times stronger than the same size of iron rope. Pretty amazing.

Henry doubled in size that summer. I was fascinated by the most incredible design he had on his back. I'd watch him work with what looked like black and shiny fangs. He kept them tucked under his chin, using them like pincers. Henry simultaneously enthralled and repelled me. But I grew to love that little eight-legged creepy-crawly. He taught me lessons I never expected to learn from a spider.

Henry Taught Me About Balance

I learned an important life lesson from Henry when a leaf blew into his web. He scurried to seize it, render it immobile, and wrap it up for a midnight feast. The only problem he had was finding a place to start wrapping. I watched as he went over and over that maple leaf. He probed every contour and notch with his front legs and fangs. Tenaciously, he moved all around the edges of the leaf, down the stem, then up and around, again and again. Finally, he gave up on being able to package the leaf for a later meal and returned to his corner.

Since spiderwebs are very sticky, I guessed that poor Henry would have to blast that leaf out somehow, then spend all night darning the resulting hole. It was only a few minutes later when I noticed that the leaf had vanished and Henry was snoozing quietly in his corner. In a very balanced move, after he'd done his best, Henry just left the leaf alone and let nature take its course by blowing it away for him.

I thought about Henry and the leaf the next time I became confused. Like Henry, I persisted until I was satisfied that no more could be done, then I returned to my corner knowing that the universe takes care of such things. Yes, indeed.

Henry Knew When a Job Was Finished

One evening I noticed that Henry wasn't in his web! Panic-stricken, I leaped onto our couch for a closer look. Sure enough, Henry was gone. I called my husband, as if he could do something. I frantically scanned the windowsill for signs of Henry. Thankfully, there he was, groping along the windowsill acting stunned, not his agile self. I couldn't bear to watch, so I closed the drapes and hoped for the best. About five minutes went by and that silly spider was back in his web. It must have been spider luck.

That was the beginning of the end of Henry's visit. Autumn

was nearing and the weather became colder. Then one day, not too long after he'd fallen, Henry left his web in tatters. We never saw him again. His lean-to way up in the corner of the window remained throughout the winter. I'd have taken a broom after anyone who disturbed it. I don't know what happens to spiders during the winter, but I guess that Henry crawled down to Mother Earth, where he covered himself for his final nap.

I often remember the special summer Henry came to stay. And how he worked with me in his spider way to weave a web of creativity where I could dream my dreams.

A Web to Spin: Are there angel animals (and insects) who could show you how to tap into your own creativity? Could they be as close as your backyard or window? Take a look!

Kurt, who lives in Armada, Michigan, works as a handyman at an antique store where he feeds twelve pets and helps with daily chores. After Kurt graduates from high school, he plans to study computer science. Kurt runs his own web site dedicated to providing information to people about deer. In this story, Kurt shares how angel animals inspired him to follow his dreams.

The Deer Helped Me Win a College Scholarship

KURT D. WELCH

In late September of 1994 I took a walk behind my house to see if there were any good hunting places for the upcoming bow season. In a small fallow field of about five acres, I spotted half a dozen deer grazing. After bow season began, I decided to try hunting in the small weedy field.

The first couple of nights I didn't see anything, but after the third night, I saw a few deer. Then the next night I noticed a couple more. By the end of the first week, I began seeing deer nearly every night. I enjoyed watching the deer so much that I never even thought about drawing my bow.

I started a pattern of returning to the field each night, no matter how bad the weather was, even when I was sick. Being with the deer gave me a complete happiness that I'd never felt before. I hadn't known I could be so peaceful and wondered if I'd ever feel this good again. It was almost as if the deer were coming to that field to make me happy, because seeing deer nearly every night for three months is highly unusual, especially during hunting season. It seemed like nature's gift to me.

A Powerful Gift

The power of this gift became most apparent on the night of January 1, 1995, the final day of bow season. It also turned out to be the most influential day of my life. I didn't expect to see any deer because the night before there had been a harsh winter storm, which covered the landscape with a thick layer of ice and snow. The wind chill felt as if it were below zero.

Determined to see deer once more, I walked on the crunchy snow to the field. As I sat in the field I thought, *Well, nature, what's this new year going to bring?* After waiting for about an hour, I still hadn't seen any deer and thought about leaving.

To my surprise, I detected movement on the other side of the field. I looked through my binoculars and identified the object as a doe. The doe walked slowly in my direction, stopping every couple of paces until she stood about twenty yards away. Then she looked in my direction, just staring at me. She could smell me because the wind blew in her direction, but she didn't run.

I suddenly realized that I was smiling. Never in my whole life had I been so happy! I believed that this doe, whom I think of as an angel, came to the field that day to make me happy once more, as the deer had done hundreds of times before her.

In this instant, I began reflecting on how much I'd enjoyed this field. I knew my happiness was nearing an end, because the development of houses threatened to take the land away. I didn't want my peaceful days with the deer to be over forever. That night, I made a promise and a dream began to form in my heart. I decided that I'd start doing better in school so I could get a good job. I'd earn enough money to buy my own field where the deer could graze and then I could re-create the special days we'd had together. Eager to carry out my new mission, I ran home and immediately went to work.

Would My Dream Come True?

Only time would tell if my dream was merely a teenager's fleeting fantasy or if my motivation and my New Year's resolution were truly strong. The first evidence showed up on my next report card. I had made the highest grades. I've never been a bad student, but it was out of the ordinary for me to get A's in all of my classes. And that was only the beginning. Ever since the night when I made my promise to the deer and myself, I've gotten all A's and A+'s and have earned dozens of scholastic awards. I rose to the rank of second in my class and began teaching myself skills outside of school, such as computer programming. In my senior year I received a full-tuition college scholarship for academic excellence worth more than $45,000!

When people ask what inspired my academic achievements, I tell them that my parents have motivated me. This is true. But I know that the deer gave me my greatest reasons for succeeding. Ever since that New Year's Day when I stood in the field, with gratitude in my heart for the doe who came to give me a final moment of peace and happiness, I've kept my promise and will continue to do so until I am once again reunited with my deer.

Thoughts for a Day in the Field: Are there opportunities for you to have a relationship with an angel animal in nature? Might an angel animal in the wild inspire you to preserve a space where you can enjoy peace and happiness together?

Linda is self-employed. She enjoys volunteering for her church in Red Deer, Alberta, Canada. She says that her animal companion, an eight-year-old sheltie named Lady with a gentle face and soft eyes, is a special creature. She introduces us to a way of forming families— brothers and sisters who help each other in the tough times—by matching abandoned angel animals with spiritually needy youngsters.

"Throwaway" Kids and "Throwaway" Animals Found Each Other

LINDA LANSDELL

A few years ago I taught emotionally disturbed teens in a group home. My students, all in crisis situations, could be there for a day, a week, or months. Many of them required our lockup facility so they wouldn't harm themselves or others.

These very tough kids—some were prostitutes or drug users— often came directly from prison to my classroom. They were society's "throwaway" kids—youngsters without homes, street children bereft of families to love and care for them. They suffered from severe emotional problems. In the classroom I could see that their hearts were broken. Desperately, they needed to receive love but, more importantly, they needed to give it.

I found ways for my kids to help around the classroom and to tutor each other. Their self-worth grew as they gave of themselves. I always marveled at how, when offered the opportunity, they'd open their hearts and take pride in doing a job well. No one seemed to want or need them. Yet, it was amazing how responsibly they'd act when they felt needed.

A Plan for Giving and Receiving

One summer a friend mentioned an idea that I thought would be a great program for my students. They could volunteer to help at our local animal shelter.

I called the director of the shelter and proposed that my kids offer their services. The director immediately liked the idea. Here was an opportunity for homeless, abused teens with broken hearts to meet homeless, abused animals with broken hearts. I never imagined how beneficial the relationships between these kindred spirits would be!

The plan was simple. We arranged that every Wednesday morning I'd bring over my little crew and they'd shovel waste, clean the runs, wash dog and cat bowls, and feed the animals.

But then came the risky part of the program.

After chores, the youngsters would earn the freedom to walk one of the dogs in the wooded area behind the shelter. Their walk together would be unsupervised.

Students often ran away from our group home. Yet, here I was handing them the freedom and responsibility of walking from the shelter into a wooded area where I couldn't even see them.

Could they handle it? Would any of them run away?

We Began the Project

The group home staff helped me work out standards students would need to meet each week if they were to go to the animal shelter. We all agreed that this was an unusual program, but everyone was willing to try it. The payoff could be wonderful, if it worked.

So, each week on Wednesday morning the staff and I carefully went over the list of students who had met the requirements. All week, students worked hard to curb their tempers, be cooperative, and get their schoolwork completed so they could have a morning with the animals.

Those who qualified were driven to the animal shelter for a morning of serving and loving something beyond themselves. At the shelter they saw animals who had been mistreated and abandoned. The kids quickly made the analogy that this place was a group home for animals, just as their group home housed kids who had been hurt and rejected. It was amazing to see how even the most hardened, tough kids understood the animals' loneliness and pain at not having a loving home of their own.

I emphasized to my students how much the animals needed their love and care. For some kids, it was a slow process and others took to the idea immediately. Soon, most of them were opening their hearts to the abused animals. They took pride in themselves and the kind of job they did because they knew the animals needed them. We focused on helping the students give of themselves. As they served the animals, the youngsters were transforming before our eyes. We watched them learning how to accept unconditional love from the dogs and cats.

I especially noticed the changes that were happening in my students one day when a very special rabbit was brought into the shelter while they worked. The kids were horrified at the sight of this poor creature. He'd been dipped into a barrel of oil and left unable to move. The little rabbit could barely breathe. He was completely soaked, his eyes painfully filled with oil.

Suddenly, even the most self-centered troublemakers among our group were consumed with concern for the rabbit. They asked a thousand questions and hovered around the staff as they worked to save the animal. For the next week, they kept asking me to call to find out how the rabbit was doing.

We Matched the Timid with the Shy

Perhaps one of the sweetest examples of the miraculous growth that was occurring came to the surface when I'd pick out a very shy, withdrawn student and ask for his help. The shelter director would point out an animal who needed extra loving care. Then we'd ask the student if he'd spend time loving and helping the animal to trust people again.

Slowly, the youngster and animal would relate to each other. The student would timidly talk to the animal, encouraging him with toys and eventually brush the animal or sit beside him. We'd watch in amazement as, time and again, a withdrawn youngster and a scared animal would tenderly give each other comfort and warmth during their darkest times.

One of my most memorable experiences in this remarkable program involved Tim (not his real name). Tim, a teenager who had been in the home for several weeks, had a gentle face, but his family life and difficulties in school left him stubborn, extremely uncooperative, and negative. Yet, at the animal shelter Tim shone. He was caring and gentle. He did his tasks and seemed to have a natural ability for working with the animals.

Each Wednesday, Tim earned the right to go to the shelter. Then I noticed that his cooperative ways with the animals began to transfer to other areas of his life. Tim began to trust that no matter what he did, I'd never give up on him, and somehow, he'd be able to bounce back from tough times. If he had a rough morning, he'd come back after lunch, put in a great afternoon, and wipe the slate clean, earning his way toward going to the shelter that week.

Tim was typical of students who began to respect themselves as they gave to the animals. They were feeling successful; they were starting to trust; and they were gaining that irreplaceable thrill of being needed and responsible.

The Students Created Better Lives for Themselves

These troubled kids saw that the animals were lonely and desperate for love and attention. For maybe the first time in their lives, someone said to them, "Can you help?" My kids learned that chores came first and then they could play, walk, and spend time with the animals. They learned to take pride in volunteering and this gave them a glimpse of good citizenship. Never before had they been considered contributing members of society. Yet, these kids begged to volunteer at the shelter.

To heighten the learning value of the shelter visits, the director of the shelter came to our group home and taught about responsible pet ownership. She explained how to provide a loving home for an animal. We hoped that hearing what animals need for nurturing and growth would introduce our students to principles of responsible care in a healthy home.

The director showed the students graphic pictures of animal abuse and neglect that touched even the young males, who had done time in prison and were proud of it. It wasn't unusual to see them quickly brush away tears. Later, they'd write in their daily journals for me to read about feelings that were too private and tender for them to express openly. The director's visits and their growing concern for the animals opened a small window for my kids to face the pain and shame they'd endured as survivors of abuse. Some students even did artwork for the shelter and wrote poems trying to express the animals' inner feelings and yearning for loving families.

Amazing Results

In the three years we ran the program I marveled at how these homeless animals, carelessly thrown away, were beautiful souls who played such important roles in the lives of my kids. All the animals served to touch these young hearts, opening them to give and receive love.

As we had planned, my students walked the dogs, unsupervised, in the woods for up to a half hour. They could have easily escaped into the safety of the thick trees. I impressed on each of them my trust and respect that they'd bring back the animal in their care safely and on time.

Remarkably, I never lost a student or an animal.

The animals at this shelter and the students in my classroom showed me that when "throwaway" kids and "throwaway" animals give and receive love from each other, they form relationships and families that help them to survive. The world may have forgotten about and not needed my kids, but the animals sure did. These shining angel animals showed some very needy kids the way back home from heartbreak and abuse.

A Tail to Wag: Has this story inspired you to give of yourself by volunteering at an animal shelter or by helping abused and needy children in some way? Could you reap the spiritual benefits of mending the heart or easing the pain of a "throwaway" animal or a "throwaway" kid?

Judy volunteers by donating her art and craft projects for sale at the
Ronald McDonald House to help sick children. She and her husband,
who live in Glen Easton, West Virginia, currently have a fourteen-
bird family. Her story shows how an angel animal launched her on
a project that has brought great happiness, healing, and uncondi-
tional love.

A Bird Helped Me Discover the Purpose of My Life

Judy Fay McLaughlin

More than three years ago I was diagnosed with a medical problem that the doctors said would shorten my life span, eventually
cripple me until I needed a wheelchair, and then cause me to become bedridden. I was always very active, playing softball in
three leagues, bowling in tournaments, traveling to clog dances
to entertain people, and engaging in many types of physical exercise and sports. I also helped my husband with the physically demanding job of remodeling our home. The news that I'd lose the
ability to do so many things I enjoyed upset me very much.
I knew that the activities I loved would cause me severe pain so
I became very depressed. I asked God why I was on this earth,
if the only experience left for me was to go through so much
suffering.

For a long time, I thought God had no answer for my question.

One day my husband came home from the local flea market
and asked me to ride with him to shop for an air conditioner. At
that time I wouldn't leave the house except for doctor's office visits. I'd become very depressed and didn't want to get out of bed. I

told my husband to go without me, but that day he persisted until I joined him.

When we got to the flea market, I saw the prettiest African grey Timneh. Ever since I was a little girl, I'd wanted an African grey bird and a cockatoo. When I talked to this bird, named Coa Coa, I could see that he was very unhappy and I felt sorry for him. The lady who was selling the bird let me take him out of his cage and handle him. In response to my attention, Coa Coa bit me hard. When my husband asked if I was ready to leave, I said good-bye to Coa Coa and went to the car, where I waited for him to finish shopping. Suddenly, there was my husband holding a birdcage and asking me to help him get Coa Coa into the car. Then he grinned and said, "This is our new air conditioner." The thoughtfulness and caring he showed by getting me the type of bird that I'd wanted all my life brought tears to my eyes.

Coa Coa Was Afraid Too

I fell in love with Coa Coa right away. But in only one hour I realized that something was wrong with him. He'd run from me and bite. He acted crazy. I thought he was reacting to all the changes, but later, when he still hadn't adjusted to his new home, I did some research into his background. Within a few days I learned a lot about Coa Coa. He'd been caught in the wild and brought to the United States. It was amazing that he survived the trip. Only about two out of ten captured birds live through such an ordeal. He'd also been in several homes, and it seemed as if he'd been badly mistreated. Because he was so afraid, he snapped constantly and I often needed stitches to heal from his bites. Everyone I talked to about Coa Coa advised me that this situation would never change; they all said I should destroy the bird.

Their well-meant words didn't comfort me; instead, I felt angry. It seemed as if both Coa Coa and I were no longer what others thought we should be. I had to face the fear of living with physical disability, and Coa Coa needed to overcome his fear of humans. I decided not to give up on him.

With much love and patience, Coa Coa began to bond with me. He started to call me Mommy and would run around the house looking for me. He wouldn't let me handle him, although he was always glad to see me. Eventually Coa Coa started giving me kisses and talking constantly. If he couldn't find me when I was trying to do housework, he'd run down the hall yelling, "Mommy, Mommy! Where are you? I love you. Come get me, please."

Coa Coa Spreads His Wings to Love Others

Gradually, by letting Coa Coa relate to me at his own pace, he became more secure. And something wonderful began happening to me. I discovered that I was no longer depressed! I realized that if this bird could learn to love me after everything he'd been through, then the least I could do would be to survive my condition. I wanted to be there for this creature who had become my best friend. But the little tyke brought me even more joy by opening my eyes to a valuable kind of work that I could do in this world.

After Coa Coa came to our home, word of how a mistreated bird had been transformed by love and caring began to spread. I started to get phone calls about other birds who had been abused. I'd listen to their sad stories and then bring these birds home with me one at a time. Currently, I have fourteen birds. "Big brother" Coa Coa now tells the others to behave and says, "Mommy will be right back."

We adopted Lefty, a very talkative African grey who is still a baby. He lets no one but my husband and me handle him. Shadow is a dusty gray conure who was kept in a back room with no company or light. He loves and preens us and every bird who comes into the house. Precious is a "pocket parrot" or parrotlet, who had never played with toys or people and was left in a cockatoo cage that was too big for such a small bird. Peaches, a baby cockatoo, had a deformed leg and was abandoned in a garage to waste away. He asks for "hugs and kisses, Mommy" and loves to feel the wind and sun. His leg was so deformed that he couldn't hold his food to eat, nor walk or stand straight. A very loving vet performed surgery, and now the joy of watching Peaches feed, preen himself, walk, and stand is thrilling. He uses his bad leg, which will never be perfect, to reach out, touch me, and say, "I love you."

Baby, a cockatiel who was lonely because her owner couldn't afford to keep her, arrived next. She constantly tells us that she's a baby girl and sings as loud as she can. Four canaries no one wanted—Ringo, Princess Di, Dusty, and Prince Charles—wake me each morning with their songs. Houdini and Harriet are love-birds who weren't wanted. Houdini was bald but is now growing feathers again. Harriet wants to mate. She's had four eggs that we hope will produce. Sam, a cockatoo, was caught in the wild. He was bald from plucking himself due to boredom and frustration. Almost all his feathers have grown back, and he enjoys playing with his new Mommy and many toys. Our last addition is Sweety, a blue-fronted Amazon given away by her previous owner be-cause she bit all the time. When she arrived at our home, she was missing two toes that *another* bird had bitten off. Sweety loves my husband so much that she lies on her back, coos for him, and says, "good girl." She hasn't bitten either one of us and is starting to play with toys. There isn't a mean bone in her body.

Giving Purpose to My Life

To keep me near all my kids and allow me to spend time lov-ing them, I now crochet, knit, do plastic canvas, and quilt. (My bird family loves to try to run down the hall with my quilts in their beaks.) I've started teaching crafts to others. I give hand-worked gifts to my family, friends, and charity organizations. These activities, which keep me close to my birds, have given new meaning to my life.

But I feel that the greatest reason for my being on this earth is to save these mistreated birds from a life of neglect and abuse. Several people in my neighborhood have been inspired by the joy and purpose caring for the birds has brought to my life and are now trying to do the same thing. Although I cry when I see mistreated birds, it gives me comfort to know that there are other people who will care for and love them.

It's expensive and time-consuming to feed and clean the birds, but the joy is unbelievable when I see a bird who once sat in one spot and never moved start to talk, sing, play, and be excited to see me when I enter the room.

I no longer feel useless. As long as my body holds out, I'll try to help as many of the birds as I can. I thank God for giving me the chance to assist His little miracles and for the joy they bring me. But most of all I thank Coa Coa for showing me the way.

My husband is now in the process of adding a room to our home for the birds. It will have a space where I can sit by them, with windows all around so the birds and I can look out and enjoy the world. We'll be able to watch all the wild birds that come to our yard to eat the food I put out for them.

Sometimes our home is very noisy, but it's filled with joyful sounds. I don't resent my physical condition anymore. I feel lucky that my husband has a big enough heart and the ability to build this special room for the birds. As the room is being constructed, I carry them into it, one at a time. I tell them that they are getting a new place with lots of light where they can move around easily. I think they understand what I'm saying.

Because Coa Coa opened my heart, today I'm glad to be alive and able to help birds, to hear their beautiful voices and feel their special love.

Wings to Fly: How are angel animals opening your heart, especially when you're going through tough times? Are they inspiring you to give love and service to humans as well as animals?

John is a reporter for a business publication. He writes children's books and does nature photography. John and his wife, Kay, live in Salem, Oregon, with their two cats, Max and Lucy. In his story, angel animals offer some free advice for having a better life.

A Dog and Cat Became Our Business Partners

JOHN MARIKOS

Years ago a friend brought a man to our house. Before long it became apparent that the man wanted my wife and me to sell cleaning products. This involved joining a pyramid marketing program in which he would get a percentage of every sale.

As the man pressured us to join his company, our cat, Dusty, jumped off the refrigerator about four feet away and leaped onto the dining room table. This placed Dusty between us and the man. Then our collie, Valentine, who had been sleeping about three or four feet away, woke up and landed on the same table. Demanding to be petted, Valentine also stood between us and the man.

My wife and I interpreted these actions by our animals as their playful way of protecting us. We felt that Dusty and Valentine were responding to something that wasn't right for us. They were letting us know their opinion about this project.

Later, we found out that we'd made a very good decision not to get involved with the marketing program. We realized it wouldn't have been right for our personal goals and interests. Dusty and Valentine had given us wise business advice.

An Idea to Consider: We're all aware that angel animals warn us of physical danger. But is it possible that they sense ways we could pursue a greater good? Perhaps angel animals read unconscious clues we give from our higher nature—the part of us that knows what's best for us. Maybe they mirror what we know intuitively but aren't yet recognizing. Could you discover important clues by watching signs that angel animals give?

More to Inspire You

All we humans have to do is observe the miraculous ways angel animals help us and each other and we're bound to learn how to give more love and service to all life.

Angel animals inspire us to greater good by reflecting our state of consciousness back to us. Gretchen Youngdahl, who works in human resources at a major grocery store chain distribution center, is from Alabaster, Alabama. In her story, "Migan Shows Me How to Be a Leader," Gretchen writes about how a dog helped her realize that she could adjust an attitude toward her older brother that she'd carried since childhood. She says that she'd always felt that she lagged behind her brother, struggling to follow his lead. Now, as an adult, Gretchen wanted to come from behind to establish a more mature relationship with her sibling, one that was based on mutual respect. One snowy winter day, as she and her brother walked through his farm with his dog, Migan, running ahead to make a track in the snow for her to follow, Gretchen realized that Migan mirrored back to her the secret for changing her relationship with her brother. Gretchen writes, "The dog was giving me a moment to realize the significance of being a leader, of what it meant to be responsible for showing another the way. I finally understood that all those years and times I'd been struggling to follow my big brother, he'd been walking ahead and striving to cut an easier path for me!"

Read on to discover how angel animals demonstrate coping spiritually with life's most challenging situations.

Part Two

WHAT ANGEL ANIMALS TEACH US ABOUT HANDLING LIFE'S CHALLENGES

God was angry that Balaam was going, and as Balaam was riding along on his donkey, accompanied by his two servants, the angel of the Lord stood in the road to bar his way. When the donkey saw the angel standing there holding a sword, it left the road and turned into the fields. Balaam beat the donkey and brought it back onto the road. Then the angel stood where the road narrowed between two vineyards and had a stone wall on each side. When the donkey saw the angel, it moved over against the wall and crushed Balaam's foot against it. Again, Balaam beat the donkey. Once more the angel moved ahead; he stood in a narrow place where there was no room at all to pass on either side. This time, when the donkey saw the angel, it lay down. Balaam lost his temper and began to beat the donkey with his stick. Then the Lord gave the donkey the power of speech, and it said to Balaam, "What have I done to you? Why have you beaten me these three times?"

Balaam answered, "Because you have made a fool of me! If I had a sword, I would kill you."

The donkey replied, "Am I not the same donkey on which you have ridden all your life? Have I ever treated you like this before?"

"No," he answered.

Then the Lord let Balaam see the angel standing there with his sword; and Balaam threw himself face downward on the ground. The angel demanded, "Why have you beaten your donkey three times like this? I have come to bar your way, because you should not be making this journey. But your donkey saw me and turned aside three times. If it hadn't, I would have killed you and spared the donkey."

Balaam replied, "I have sinned. I did not know that you

*were standing in the road to oppose me; but now if you think
it is wrong for me to go on, I will return home."*

—Numbers 22:22–35

The next part of this book is designed to help you reflect upon and apply the spiritual lessons angel animals teach about dealing with some of life's most difficult situations. You'll learn what the animals have to share about handling change, living healthy, letting go and trusting, and finding the mystical in the mundane. We hope that these inspiring stories will help you recognize and follow divine wisdom. These wonderful examples from angel animals have helped us become more aware of the need to a acquire a donkey's vision instead of stumbling along in spiritual blindness without seeing angels on the road.

Chapter Five

Sailing on the Winds of Change

In the last few years, science has proven what many have long believed about the transformatory power of animal–human bonding: Animals not only can make our lives better, but they can make better people of us.

—Sylvia Paine

*A*t the local animal humane society where Linda volunteers, she often witnesses how angel animals demonstrate that by listening to and trusting your heart, you'll know what changes are best for your spiritual growth. Here are a couple of her stories.

A Puppy Chooses a New Home

A Lhasa Apso puppy happily left his cage to visit with anyone who came along. A woman with two little girls spent time with this puppy and asked a lot of questions about the breed. The woman decided to put the puppy on hold so that her husband could come in later in the day to see him. While the woman filled out papers, I went to get a sign to place on the puppy's cage so he wouldn't be adopted that day. When I returned, a very nice couple had opened the cage and held their hands out for the puppy to come to them. This time, the little Lhasa plopped his rear end down stubbornly and refused to budge. I told the couple not to feel bad because it looked as if the puppy had already made his decision and he evidently didn't want to chance going home with the wrong family. Then the woman came back with her children, opened the cage, and the puppy bounded into her arms. She said that she was going to adopt him right away. I told her what had happened while she'd been away. The woman said, "I think they know these things, don't you?" I told her that I believe the animals know when they've met the right family.

The Woman Who Wanted a Barking Dog

All the volunteers at the shelter had been walking the large dogs from their kennels to outside. Most of the dogs barked vociferously. A woman came into the kennel and said, "I want a dog that barks." She hadn't said, "I want a dog to love." She appeared to need a doggie alarm system. I watched in amazement as the dogs, all of whom had been barking like crazy only moments before, became silent. The woman would pass cages and say, "He's not a barker." She left without a dog. It looked to me as if these animals, tuning in to a higher nature that knows what's best for them, had done what was necessary to keep from going home with someone who might not appreciate them.

Have Angel Animals Helped with Historical Changes?

Have animals helped with changes that have historical significance? Could animals have a purpose they fulfilled that is overlooked when we express gratitude for the contributions of the humans who were involved?

In his well-researched book *What Was the Name of Paul Revere's Horse?* Patrick Leehey tells us about the animal who helped Paul Revere carry out his goal of contacting patriot leaders Samuel Adams and John Hancock to warn them of an impending British invasion. Leehey brings attention to the fact that this event, which shaped history, was accompanied by the beat of a horse's hooves.

The stories you're about to read offer remarkable wisdom from angel animals on how they handle the winds of change, the gales that inevitably blow into your life and the lives of those you love.

Julie is a graphic artist and writer from Iowa City, Iowa. She enjoys art and nature and loves all animals, especially dogs. Julie and her husband share their home with three German shorthaired pointers named Tuza, Shanti, and Tobe. Julie's story inspires us to read signals from angel animals who let us know that it's time to make changes we've been thinking about for a long time.

A Sparrow Led Me to Volunteer

Julie Johnson Olson

One day, while driving home, I was about to turn a corner when I saw a little sparrow hopping on the road. I stopped my car in midturn, put on my blinkers because this was a busy Iowa City street, and opened the door. The little bird hopped up to my door, looked at me, and then skittered under the car. I got out and spoke to him soothingly. The sparrow seemed content listening to me talk to him.

My husband, Paul, usually keeps a clean towel in the trunk that he uses to wipe the car down after a wash. I found the towel and coaxed the bird into it, then gently wrapped the cloth around his little body. He barely moved, and for a minute, I thought he'd died. Then he fluttered a little, as if to say, "I'm okay; I'm here." But he couldn't fly at all.

I drove to a vet clinic. They suggested that I take the bird to the humane society/animal shelter just a mile a way. So I put the sparrow back into the car, and we drove there. The director of this animal shelter greeted me at the door with so much love that I knew I'd come to the right place.

It concerned me that my little buddy hadn't moved since we'd arrived at the shelter. As we entered the office area, two parakeets greeted us. The little sparrow fluttered wildly under the towel as if he wanted to see who was saying hello to him.

The director took the injured bird out of the towel and stroked his head. She put him outside where he could fly away if he felt up to it. She also gave my little friend some birdseed. She tried to reassure me by saying, "Sometimes birds hit a window and are stunned."

Did I Bring the Sparrow Here, or Had the Bird Led Me?

While the director was trying to help the sparrow, I started to come to an interesting interpretation of this situation. I love animals. They're a big part of my life. Because of this sparrow, I was now at a place where I could help animals. Volunteering would be a new way of serving life. I'd been thinking about doing this for a while. So, then and there, I signed up to volunteer with the dogs in the shelter's care. The application said "referred by" and I wrote "an injured bird."

Right away I started helping people with their dogs. One family came to the shelter to adopt a puppy. They brought their two other dogs to get them acquainted first. To see these humans and animals meeting each other was like witnessing a happy reunion. It was very gratifying to watch the new family form.

Then we all noticed the tame little sparrow hopping over to get a better look at this loving scene, as if he were drawn to all the joy. But he still couldn't fly. The director came out and scooped him up gently. She said that she'd send him to a man who rehabilitates birds.

The sparrow was on his way to the next phase of his life. And, thanks to meeting him, so was I.

Wings to Fly: Have you been thinking about making a change in your life? Julie found that an angel animal can sometimes be a messenger to help us realize that now is the time to find ways to give more love and service. Could an angel animal be trying to deliver a similar message to you?

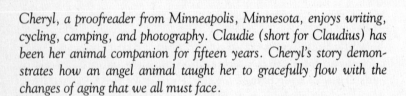

Cheryl, a proofreader from Minneapolis, Minnesota, enjoys writing, cycling, camping, and photography. Claudie (short for Claudius) has been her animal companion for fifteen years. Cheryl's story demonstrates how an angel animal taught her to gracefully flow with the changes of aging that we all must face.

My Dog Taught Me How to Age Gracefully

CHERYL L. YOCHIM

The harsh glare of artificial lights makes my eyes water and blink as I sit in the waiting room of the animal emergency clinic. My husband, on one side of me, flips through magazines. Claudie, our oversized fifteen-year-old Yorkshire terrier with beautifully flowing black and tan hair, sits on the chair at my other side. It's almost ten o'clock on Friday and we intended to spend the evening at home after a hectic week at work. Instead, we're here to find out why Claudie can't walk without losing his balance. We wait silently, having been through such emergencies several times during the last two years.

Claudie is blind and partially deaf, an insulin-dependent diabetic who has Cushing's disease. Despite his condition, this dog continues to be a golden example of how to live life with enthusiasm. We've always thought of Claudie as a child who has immeasurably improved our ability to nurture and love. But during the last few years, our little master teacher has become the aging parent, giving us lessons in how to face the latter part of life with acceptance and grace.

I Remember the Way Things Were

Too tired to read as we sit in the waiting room, I take Claudie into my arms and let him rest his head on my shoulder. Closing my eyes, I replay the evening's events.

My husband and I arrived home from work to find Claudie weaving back and forth as he stumbled down the hallway to greet us. Blind for the last year, Claudie has learned to find his way by lightly touching his forehead against a wall or piece of furniture and knowing where to go for the next several feet before touching another anchor point. Tonight, he stumbled around, searching for more anchor points than usual. I watched him carefully, knowing I'd need to clearly describe his symptoms to the receptionist at the veterinary clinic. When I called, we were told to bring Claudie in right away. My husband carried him to the car and I held him on my lap while we headed for the hospital.

In the car I closed my eyes and remembered another ride—our move from Texas to Minnesota. Claudie could still see then. He spent almost the entire three days sitting up and taking note of every car, tree, or building. I'd look back and he'd be nodding his head, eyes half-closed, a sleepy kid afraid to miss anything on such a big adventure. His love for life is always a reminder to me not to take even the simplest pleasures for granted.

During the last two years we've had to watch Claudie's health deteriorate as he ages. Yet he's adapted remarkably well at each turn. He's adjusted to twice-daily insulin injections, needles, pills, and the strange hands of vets and technicians he can only identify by smell. He doesn't try to run anymore, but he still takes every opportunity to sit in the soft grass and turn his head toward the warm sunshine. Occasionally, he lets us know when he's scared or lonely by howling if he can't find us right away. Otherwise, he's fairly content with life. He's a master at adapting to the changes of illness and aging.

Illness Hasn't Changed Claudie's Loving Ways

I float back to the waiting room. Nearby, a girl of six or seven squirms around on her knees in a chair beside her parents. The receptionist has called to them from behind a high white counter to tell the family that they'll have to wait a few more minutes. At last, though, the vet is walking a black Labrador past us to the girl and her parents. The vet tells the parents their dog has bruised and torn muscles in his hips and will take a while to heal. With the little girl and dog, the parents stand at the receptionist's counter directly in front of us to pay their bill. The dog whimpers each time he moves.

Claudie climbs down from my arms and sniffs around. Wobbling and straining his leash, he manages to nose his way into the back of the noisy Labrador. When he smells the injured Lab, Claudie licks the dog's back to offer comfort. I'm amazed to watch the big heart of my little guy. With all of his own troubles, Claudie still wants to help ease another animal's pain in whatever way he can.

At this moment I'm acutely aware that Claudie's health will continue to deteriorate as he ages. Yet, suddenly I look at our little family and feel content with my life. Claudie is helping me to be at peace during these trying experiences because, in the midst of them, he shows me where the precious gems of kindness, caring, and love are hidden. I feel as though my husband and I are being prepared in small ways now for the inevitable changes that will come for us as we and Claudie grow older. I vow to cope with changes with awareness and goodwill, as Claudie does.

The black Lab leaves. It's finally our turn. After we meet the vet, he says that the test results are unclear. It's probably an inner ear infection. With medication, Claudie should be fine. Relieved, we go to pay the bill.

Now, a woman and her two tearful teenage daughters pour through the front door with a puppy in their arms. As I look at Claudie, I think of his blind eyes that see more than mine sometimes. And I wonder if this family is aware of the spiritual gems that life is giving them at this moment.

A Tail to Wag: Cheryl beautifully points out the hidden spiritual growth that is buried like gems in the changes brought about by aging and loss of health. Are angel animals somehow demonstrating for you how to cope with changes through acceptance, graciousness, and compassion for others?

Sally is from Philadelphia, Pennsylvania. She says that she's a vege-
tarian and animal rights advocate who daily thanks animals for the
changes they make in her life. Sally and her husband, Sandy, live with
four former shelter (or stray) cats: Hocus, Pocus, Ziggy, and Shadow.
Her story reminds us that angel animals help us deal with some of life's
most difficult changes.

An Angel Without Wings Restored My Spiritual Sight

SALLY ROSENTHAL

"Of course there are angels," said one of the two clergymen who
are frequent commentators on spirituality for the national morning news show I like to watch. "Sometimes," the other cleric
added, "even people are really our angels." Looking at Shadow,
the ginger tabby who lay sleeping on the sofa beside me, I added,
"And animals."

My life had taken a difficult turn when Shadow, a former stray
cat, appeared on our patio two years earlier. At the time I met him,
I wasn't looking for a fourth cat, or an angel. But I needed one.

I had started losing my vision. This made it necessary for me
to leave a career in occupational therapy at a local psychiatric
hospital, and I missed my role as nurturer. My resilience ebbed
daily. It was hard adjusting to my changing identity and believing
in my own worth. I certainly wasn't ready to accept the esoteric
idea that angels could help me with the changes I faced.

Around this time of transition, a neighbor reported seeing a
stray cat. I decided to set out bowls of food and water. Each
morning, the bowls were spotlessly clean, but I hadn't yet seen

my elusive visitor. Occasionally, I saw a blur streak through a bush. *Is this a shadow or the stray?* I wondered. With my vision deteriorating, I couldn't be sure. Then one morning a cat purred and brushed against my legs as I filled the bowls.

My Visitor Lets Me See Him

When he finally let me see his rough, dirty fur, the timid creature might have been charitably described as "ordinary." But I knew intuitively from our first meeting that this cat was special. He began to appear, as if out of nowhere, when I opened the front door. When he became comfortable around me, he even welcomed gentle stroking. He seemed to sense that I couldn't see him clearly because he always signaled his presence with a meow or physical contact. Then he started the routine of following me when I walked around our condominium complex. And I began to wonder, *Who is the real caretaker in this relationship?*

This cat seemed to know what I wanted him to do before I mentioned it. If he followed my husband and me to our car, I asked him to return to the lawn and stay safely out of traffic's way. Much to my husband's amazement, the stray cat trotted back to the grass and curled up. I began to suspect that the cat, who now answered to Shadow, had a plan, and that plan included me.

Shadow Adopted Me

I worried about Shadow when he wasn't around. I didn't think that I could bring a feral cat indoors with three pampered house cats. Each night when Shadow appeared on our patio to say good night, I wondered if he'd be safe and if I'd find him sitting by the bowls the next morning. Then I noticed that Shadow was inspiring even more uncharacteristic behavior in me. I found myself stroking his head each night and saying to him, "Go with God, Shadow."

In the mornings, as he waited patiently for me to fill his bowls, Shadow tried to reassure me that he was hale and hardy with a purr or a thrust of his head into my hand. We kept up this routine until one cool autumn Saturday. On that day, Shadow rode quietly in his new cat carrier to the vet's for a checkup and vaccinations. Now, it was his turn to adapt to a major life change, because Shadow was moving indoors.

At a time when the traumatic physical changes in my life caused me to think I had little to give, Shadow taught me that I could still nurture. I believe that his adjustment to indoor life was natural and relatively easy because, after all, he was meant to be there.

Shadow found a way to remind me about his role in my life. I mentioned at the beginning of this story that I listened to a national news program in which the clerics talked about angels. I scratched Shadow's head that morning as I turned off the television and asked him, "Do you remember when I used to say, 'Go with God, Shadow'?"

His response to my question astounded me.

Shadow opened his eyes and gazed solemnly at me for a moment. Then he stretched a paw and placed it gently on my heart. And I wondered how I could once not have believed in angels. Especially ones whose wings are hidden beneath fur.

A Paw to Lick: Could you use Sally's blessing, "Go with God, Shadow"? Is there someone—human or animal—who draws from your heart a capacity for caring and nurturing that you didn't realize was there?

Rona is a holistic therapist and a reader for a publishing house who lives in London, England. She entertains children at parties by dressing as a clown, doing magic tricks, and teaching gymnastics. Tigger and Bonnie are her two cat companions. Bonnie helped her witness a miracle.

A Cat That Love Transformed

RONA HARDING

Three years ago my daughter and I wondered what we could do that would bring more love to the world. How could we serve life?

We decided to visit the RSPCA (Royal Society for the Prevention of Cruelty to Animals) and give some love to the animals who were without homes. While we visited the animal shelter, a pretty cat with lime-green eyes came up and began to dance for us. She'd been left at the RSPCA when she was nine months old and had been there for a few months. The staff told us that this cat was half wild, and they were having trouble finding a home for her. We left the RSPCA wishing we could help. We phoned lots of friends but no one could adopt her.

We went back to the RSPCA for a visit. During this time my daughter had been having problems at school and the stress caused her to suffer from chest pains. When we arrived at the animal shelter, we didn't see the cat with the lime-green eyes. But when my daughter called for her, the cat came running, doing her little dance again. My daughter asked her father if we could keep the cat. He agreed immediately and her chest pains disappeared instantly.

The RSPCA warned us that because the cat was half wild anyone who took her home would only be able to give to the animal and would receive nothing in return. They usually put a microchip in the neck of each animal to make it easier to return lost pets to their homes, and give them vaccinations. The staff said that the little cat, whom we named Bonnie, might not let them come close enough to do these procedures. They approached wearing thick gloves and carrying a blanket to throw over her. To their amazement, Bonnie stayed quite still. It was as if she knew that we had fallen in love with her at first sight and in spite of her previous problems, she was coming home with us.

Bonnie Adjusted to Her New Home

We put Bonnie in the living room on the first day in her new home. She took refuge under a table. Bonnie was scared of everyone and everything. Then we took one of our other cats to meet her. Bonnie came out from under the table and instantly fell in love with Tigger, our big ginger cat. Tigger was shocked because most other animals rejected his love. We were witnessing the start of a lifelong friendship between these two creatures.

On the second day after we brought Bonnie home, we couldn't find her. I eventually tracked her to where she was hiding—up the chimney. I put on a clown wig so I wouldn't get soot all over my head and managed to coax her down. As soon as she saw me in the strange wig, Bonnie darted back up the chimney. So I left some fish in the room to entice her to come out. Later that day we found Bonnie covered in black soot back under the table, but she'd left no footprints on the cream-colored carpet and walls of the living room! It took three of us a long time to bathe her while playing relaxing music so she wouldn't scratch or bite.

Life continued on an even keel until the day before Bonnie was scheduled to have her sterilization operation. She disappeared. I sent her a message with my mind: "If you want to live with us, you'll need to have this operation." She returned the next day.

It has taken three years for Bonnie to allow us to stroke her and pick her up. She still gets frightened by sudden movements. Yet, I believe what we have witnessed is a miracle: a total transformation. Bonnie has taught us patience. It's been such a healing experience to share our lives with her. I've learned from Bonnie that nothing is ever totally damaged. With love, anything can be made whole.

A Paw to Lick: Bonnie had to go through tremendous changes, but her story shows that no matter how much fear you feel, love can overcome it. Is there an animal or human in your life whose heart is closed by fear or anger? Can you offer the kind of love that helps others cope with their rapidly changing world?

Jane, who lives in Minneapolis, graduated from the University of Minnesota close to the year she celebrated her fiftieth birthday. She loves singing, square dancing, writing, walking, and working with the dogs who are her constant companions. Fuller, her new honey-gold retriever guide dog, works with her throughout days full of country roads, city streets, crowds, traffic, all kinds of weather conditions, and life-making moments. Jane's story introduces us to an angel animal who shows us how to handle the changes that come with retiring from work.

Baxter Retires

JANE L. TOLENO

My twin sister and I are legally blind because of an in-hospital accident following our premature births. Until I was thirty-seven years old I used long white canes as mobility aids. With my favorite cane, Abel by name, I traveled successfully and happily throughout the United States and several Canadian provinces.

My husband, two children, and I settled in the Minneapolis suburbs when I turned thirty-three. All at once everything was new to me. Over time, after gathering much information, I decided to switch from using white canes to working with guide dogs. Others have written about the remarkable work guide dogs and their partners do together. But guide dogs retire when their working days are over. Although every working dog's needs in retirement are unique, I want to share the story of how my second guide dog, Baxter, a black Labrador, and I made it through the new territory called "transition." Together we learned how to transform him from being an excellent working dog to a free and happily retired family dog. Perhaps Baxter's story will help others who are making a change from going to a daily job to enjoying their days without working.

Baxter's physical work noticeably slowed during his seventh and eighth working years. It would have been unfair, irresponsible, and unsafe for us to continue working together. Yet his eagerness and joy remained undiminished and his determined, savvy, street-smart self was as big and bold as ever. Baxter's bighearted giving to me challenged me to give right back to him. But even though it was difficult to think of being without him, I knew that I had to accept the responsibility of freeing him. If he stayed with me, he'd want to work, and this just wasn't possible anymore. My dream and goal were to help Baxter learn how to play and become a new family's beloved pet.

It Was Time to Find Baxter's Retirement Home

First, I listed all the things Baxter loved to do for play when he was off work. Next, I asked other guide dog users to tell me their stories of retiring their constant companions and guides. Then I asked my family and close friends to imagine what kind of home would be perfect for Baxter. I called everyone who had offered over the years to give Baxter a home if I ever needed to retire him as my guide dog. During Baxter's eighth spring and summer we visited several families and exchanged information about Baxter's routines, schedules, and, of course, his favorite treats and ways of playing. Through this interview process, it gradually became clear which home would be the best match for Baxter.

We visited Baxter's prospective family in their home. Afterward, they invited him to go places with them without his harness on, while I participated simply as one of their group. Next, he went with the family and stayed at their home for a visit. After these experiences, all five family members asked questions about Baxter. They began to feel special about their individual and shared relationships with him. I spent time with adults in the family, showing them how to work with Baxter on a leash, do obedience commands, and to express their love while grooming him. The children and I played and shared the adventure of helping them get to know their new dog. The family shared my tears and held my hands as I gathered the courage to let them adopt Baxter.

Then the day of transition arrived. The new family's van pulled into our driveway. With a mix of emotions, we all felt the awesome significance of having reached the culmination of this yearlong transition. I asked, "Do any of us have questions, concerns, or last-minute fears?" The silence that greeted my question meant a resounding, "No!" They were ready to permanently welcome Baxter into their home. The doors to their van slid open. Baxter hopped into it without any hesitation. They drove away, and I was left to deal with loving and missing my wonderful dog, yet filled with the gratitude that he'd been able to find such a wonderful place to retire.

I sometimes get updates from the family about how Baxter is doing. His new family is coaxing him to hide less during thunderstorms. When I heard this news, I thought, *Isn't that the best? Baxter has shown that it's possible to have fewer fears when you retire than you had during your working life.* If only everyone could make transitions in their old age with such dignity and grace.

A Tail to Wag: Does Baxter's story give you any clues to making changes in your own life? Are there ways you could make transitions that would enable you to ease into them gradually, letting go of the old and being grateful for new opportunities?

Mary Elizabeth's story "Sharing Grief with Joey" appears in chapter 1. This story presents us with an angel animal who found a very creative way to bring about a change in her life.

Tanja's Secret Doorway to Freedom

M. E. MARTUCCI, PH.D.

Tanja taught me that secondhand dogs need special care. They require more of everything—food, grooming, attention, and, most of all, love. Secondhand dogs, whether they come from a shelter, the street, or a friend, have been uprooted and carry a deep hurt inside.

Tanja came to live with me when she was three years old after her owners had moved out of town. She was a mixed breed, part German shepherd and part hunting dog. She had the most beautiful, soulful eyes, which seemed to reflect a longing or loneliness that I attributed to missing her former humans. I agreed to take Tanja because of her strong, protective instincts and her quiet, gentle nature.

Since I often worked late hours during the week and occasionally on weekends, I wanted a dog like Tanja. Her house was placed in my two-car garage, where she had the freedom to move around. I provided her with plenty of food and water. The back door of the garage opened onto a small deck. On warm days, I left the screened door open so Tanja could enjoy the scenery from the safety of her house.

Tanja's "Twin" Began to Explore the Neighborhood

Tanja had been with me for several weeks when my next-door neighbor told me that she'd seen the dog running through our neighborhood. I thanked my neighbor for her concern, adding quickly that she must be mistaken because Tanja was always waiting for my return home by her house inside the garage.

When I went to work, I entered and left through the garage, using the button on the wall to open and close the door. Every day Tanja watched me follow my routine and, as the garage door slowly closed, she'd walk away toward her house.

A few more weeks passed and my neighbor insisted that she'd seen Tanja walking around the neighborhood. She brought another neighbor from several houses away to confirm the Tanja sightings. I still couldn't believe it. There was no way Tanja could be loose all day and waiting where I'd left her when I returned home each night.

Then, I stayed home from work one week and discovered Tanja's secret.

The first day at home, I heard what sounded like the garage door going up. I quickly went out to keep Tanja from running away. To my surprise, Tanja stood upright on the steps but didn't look as if she intended to run away. I hit the button to close the garage door thinking that, as happened sometimes, the electronic impulse from a passing airplane might have caused the door to go up.

The next day, I glanced out my window and noticed my neighbor's garage door and mine opening simultaneously. I felt pleased to have solved the mystery. My neighbor and I had similar garage door code numbers and hers must be opening my door also. Perhaps Tanja had run out if the door had magically opened for her.

The following day, however, I heard the garage door open again. This time, my neighbor was nowhere in sight and there was no plane overhead.

When I checked on Tanja, I found her standing upright on the steps with one paw on the wall and the other front paw pressing the garage door button. Caught in the act, Tanja promptly dropped to the floor and sheepishly crawled into her house. Those soulful eyes tugged at me. I just couldn't reprimand her. Actually, I felt proud of her intelligence and initiative. Tanja had learned how to get in and out of the garage without my ever knowing it. Even more surprising was the fact that she'd left and returned within the hours I was away. When I watched her perform this feat the next day, I knew it was no fluke. Tanja had discovered how to have more freedom than I'd ever imagined.

Tanja Earned Her Freedom

Unfortunately, my residential neighborhood didn't allow for such ingenuity in pets. "All dogs must be leashed and attended by their owners," read the restrictions. Now that Tanja's secret was known, the neighborhood watch wasn't impressed or sympathetic. So, Tanja and I had to find a new home for her where she could run and play. I wasn't happy with the decision, but I knew that Tanja needed her freedom.

Now when I visit Tanja in her new home, those beautiful eyes are brighter and less soulful. Tanja's spirit is renewed and she seems content. I know she's forgiven me for not keeping her, and I'm pleased. I'll always remember the lesson she taught me: No matter how lovely your circumstances in confinement might be, you'll always want to make the changes necessary to find freedom.

A Tail to Wag: Does something deep inside call us to live our lives more simply with joy, spiritual purpose, and peace? Do we yearn for the freedom to be special and unique? What is the garage door button that your secret self longs to push? The one that will open a door to making the changes that enable you to become all you were meant to be?

More Changes

Annie Holbrook writes in her story, "Adversity Draws My Cat Family Together," about a benefit that unexpected change brought to the animals in her home in County Dublin, Ireland. "A couple of weeks ago, a stray dog got caught in a gate down the road and we called the fire brigade. When they got him out, he lived at our house until we found his owner. Our cats had to stay outside on the terrace for a couple of days and that nearly broke our hearts. We found them all cuddled together. They'd never done that inside the house. A couple of days after bringing them in, I pondered what the spiritual lesson was for me in this situation. Then I realized that the lesson had been for the cats. This sudden change in their lives caused them to bond as a family."

It seems that angel animals can show us how to use change for growing into more loving beings.

Don't Be a Victim of Change

Angel animals seem to have a pretty clear idea of what changes they will or won't accept, and many of them communicate their wishes to humans who are willing to listen. In "Tomo Takes Charge of Change in His Life," Robin McBride shows that angel animals can be included in decisions that affect them. Robin, a desktop publisher/graphic designer from Tucson, Arizona, explains how her cat, Tomo, let her and her husband, Ray, know how he felt about a proposed move.

Tomo had been very attached to his brother, Toby, who lived with Robin's sister. So, when Robin and Ray decided to move to a small town on the Oregon coast, they assumed that Tomo wouldn't want to go with them. But Tomo had other ideas. One morning, while Robin watched the cat from the kitchen window overlooking her backyard, she writes, "Tomo looked at me directly in the eyes and communicated with great authority. His 'words' filled my head. He said, 'Take me with you!' " After Tomo repeated his request, Robin assured the cat that he'd be welcome to make the move. From that day, Robin says, Tomo loosened his ties with Toby and started spending more time with her, expressing his love and letting her know that he didn't plan to be a victim of change.

In the next chapter, we think that you'll enjoy reading more on what angel animals teach us about living healthier, and about the miracles of love and compassion they bring to the lives of humans and other animals who are suffering and in pain.

Chapter Six

Living Healthy

Maybe,
a little,
like meeting God
through feather, fur, or fluttery thing.
To be judged not by words
but for the timbre of my voice.
Not by ability
but for gentleness of my touch.
And not for knowledge,
but by the Light that shines from my eyes.
To be loved
for the nature of my heart.

—Sharon Kunin,
"Could It Be?"

*A*ngel animals teach us how to become healthier and to heal in more ways than a book of this size can present. Jane Durst-Pulkys, a caterer and mother of three from Scarborough, Ontario, writes in her story, "Simba Takes Away the Pain," about the healing energy of a special cat. "Simba has something to teach us, and it is love. When you're feeling down, he seems to know something is wrong and he'll curl up in your lap. If you have any aches or pains, he lies on that part of your body and purrs like he's pulling the pain out."

Jane's observation is shared by animal lovers the world over. Angel animals just seem to know when you need help and they provide it with such graciousness.

Learning the Rhythms of Life

Angel animals bring the spiritual quality of healthy balance into our lives. They teach us to run, romp, play, take naps, and pace ourselves. They also help us to heal emotionally.

Nancy Lucas Hampton, a writer from Edgewood, Kentucky, shares her story, "Kringles's Healing Licks." She writes that her mother, who was feeling displaced and lonely, moved in with her after Nancy's father died. Nancy's other new addition to her home was a kitten who was causing her old cat, Kringles, to feel that he'd been replaced. The two foundering creatures, Kringles and Nancy's mother, befriended each other. Nancy writes, "Kringles often curls into a ball in his guardian's lap and locks a paw around her arm to keep her close. While Mother was ill for a while, Kringles crouched on her pillow and licked her face and hair as if trying to heal her. Kringles's lonely heart recognized and reached out to Mother's."

We were touched and deeply moved by the remarkable ways that the angel animals you're about to meet in this chapter mended broken hearts and bodies.

Let the healing begin.

Debbie lives in Minneapolis, Minnesota, with her husband, Myron, and two cats, Ardas and Tuza. She enjoys eating healthful cooking, taking walks in the country, and dancing. A writer and lecturer, Debbie is the author of two books, Think Yourself Thin *and* Think Yourself Loved. *Her story shows how angel animals can help us solve problems we didn't even know we had.*

A Kitty-Prescribed Solution

Debbie Johnson

Tuza is most definitely queen of her household. If things aren't in order, she figures out creative ways to set them right. When the cat box hasn't been scooped or another task is left undone, she lets us know that something is amiss. Tuza stands erect, with her head held high, and scolds us. Then we check feeding schedules, cat box, and water dishes to see if something isn't right. We've grown to trust Tuza's sense of order and balance.

One rainy spring day Tuza began to complain in her cat language that sounded something like, "NOOOOOOW!!" Her tone rang with pain and anguish. She continued trying to tell us something for a few days and we couldn't figure out the reason for her agitation. Since Tuza was usually very loving and quiet, aside from housekeeping complaints, we wondered if she was ill.

We'd noticed that Tuza had been having trouble jumping up on the bed and seemed to be getting older and slower than she should be for her age. We took her to a vet where Tuza had her hip adjusted. Then she seemed to be a happier cat.

A few days later, Tuza began to complain again, this time less vehemently. She was letting us know that in her good judgment, something was still wrong. My husband had been talking about putting cat enzymes in her food, since Tuza no longer had enough teeth to chew well. We gave her the enzymes and she seemed much more content (unless we forgot, and you can bet she reminded us!). Soon, Tuza's energy returned and she ran around the house again, seeming younger and more vigorous.

Tuza Started Warning Me About My Health

After Tuza's health problems cleared up, she began to work on mine. She knew how to let us know when her health was a concern. Now that she'd found her voice, Tuza used it for me.

For the last few years, I'd been feeling exhausted. Slowly, by following my doctor's advice, I'd improved my health. Even though the vitamins, enzymes, and herbs I took helped, I still felt tired most of the time. In my heart I knew that, most of all, I needed to rest. Instead, I pushed myself to keep up the obligations of a heavy book tour schedule, which involved travel, speaking engagements, book signings, media interviews, and workshops. As my energy increased, I'd work until I got overly tired again. Then I'd rest, but only for about half an hour.

Tuza decided this wouldn't do. She started herding me back to bed when she thought it was time for me to take a nap. In her cat world, nap time took up a good part of the days and nights. Her constant insistence on my resting made me realize that I had to stop this grueling pace. I decided to do no traveling, workshops, book signings, or pushing of myself for one year.

In the year I spent at home, I still worked more than was good for my health. I finally took one week to rest as often as I wanted. Tuza, in kitty heaven, slept next to me and purred.

Then I started to feel much better and thought I could go back to working a full day. Tuza knew better. She came into my office and scolded me until, to placate her, I went back to the bedroom, lay on the bed, and promptly fell asleep! Tuza knew I needed much more rest than I thought I did.

Tuza has taught me to look deeper and listen harder to my own instincts. She showed me that life is precious and I must learn to treat my body with respect, as a temple. Now my health is much better. And it's all because of one very persistent, healing kitty.

A Paw to Lick: Are there ways that angel animals could be letting you know something about your health or another problem in your life? Could Tuza's concern and awareness inspire you to find better ways to take care of the temple that is your body?

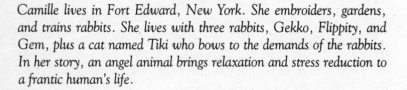

Camille lives in Fort Edward, New York. She embroiders, gardens, and trains rabbits. She lives with three rabbits, Gekko, Flippity, and Gem, plus a cat named Tiki who bows to the demands of the rabbits. In her story, an angel animal brings relaxation and stress reduction to a frantic human's life.

A Rabbit's Cure for Migraine Headaches

CAMILLE A. LUFKIN

I grew up and now live in a farm community where rabbits are outdoor pets, raised as 4-H projects, or eaten as food. Very few households around here would think of bringing a rabbit indoors, much less letting one become a member of the family. When I speak about rabbits' capacities for learning and loving, people are skeptical. "It's only a rabbit" is a phrase I hear very often.

My thoughts about rabbits were similar to those of my neighbors. That is, until a very special creature came to the pet store where I worked. A bossy, arrogant, and completely adorable rabbit with a perpetually disgruntled expression on his face changed my whole attitude. No other person or rabbit in the store liked this feisty little black, floppy-eared bunny, but he and I became friends. The rabbit reminded me of the character from a Japanese cartoon series, so I called him by the same name, Gekko.

Gekko Lived Up to His Name

The day after I named him, Gekko came home with me. In an amazingly short time, Gekko conned and danced his way into my heart and charmed my friends with his antics and personality. Soon, word spread about this incredible rabbit, and a legend built up around him that, like his Japanese cartoon character namesake, someday he was going to take over the world. Gekko's popularity spread far and wide. I even heard that people I'd never met chanted his name at science fiction conventions.

Gekko's capacity for learning seemed unlimited. He knew over two dozen obedience commands, became completely housebroken, and amused people with his mischief. Visitors to my home would greet Gekko, some even bringing "tributes" of snacks or gifts for him.

What impressed me most about Gekko was his perceptiveness. He'd already shown how lovable he was, demanding cuddles as often as he could get them, but he'd also thump his back foot whenever he thought I needed to be warned about something. He was almost delightfully jealous, shoving his way into conversations, begging for attention and acknowledgment of his great presence.

I'm most grateful to Gekko, though, for playing a crucial role in changing me from a depressed and driven person to one who lives in health, harmony, and peace. When I met Gekko, my life for the last several years had revolved from one crisis to another. I not only coped with my own problems but shared my friends' difficulties. Although a chronic pain patient, I was simultaneously trying to finish college, work two part-time jobs, and rent a corner of someone's house. I lived frantically, rarely letting myself sit still for long. Even when I'd try to spend time alone, within minutes, I'd invent a reason to run out the door.

Gekko became a sponge for my attention. I began setting time aside every day to sit the rabbit on my lap and play with him. Instead of rushing, I began to slow down my furious pace. I even started traveling with little Gekko in a pet carrier.

Very shortly after Gekko adopted me, we visited my parents in upstate New York in autumn, my favorite season. My parents own a large farmhouse with a huge yard. I put Gekko's harness on, clipped a thirty-foot rope to it, and we went outdoors.

Gekko had never seen such a large space. We explored the yard in mad-dash spurts. He danced with joy and ran faster than he'd ever been able to in our city neighborhood. Through Gekko's eyes, I relived how much I loved the home where I'd grown up. That day, I knew we could no longer be happy living in New Jersey.

Four months later, Gekko and I moved home. By spring, we had our own apartment, and Gekko bloomed into the wonderful pet I'd only seen hints of in my previous cramped living quarters.

My Lifestyle Was Ruining My Health

Even after the move, my life was still frantic. I worked at a breakneck pace and couldn't relax easily. I invited friends over most weekends, spent others with my family, and had very little time alone. I suffered from severe migraine headaches that increased in frequency. My health was getting worse.

My father had been diagnosed with cancer soon after I moved. When he became very ill, my fiancé moved from New Jersey to be with me, and I had another life to juggle with mine. I was torn between spending time with my family and saving a faltering relationship with my fiancé. The apartment seemed to shrink as I shared it with another person. Nothing in the near future looked any better.

My life became worse. During one terrible winter month, I wrecked my car in an ice storm, my father died, my fiancé and I had to move to a different home, and I got the chicken pox. For three weeks, I was too sick to do anything and too restless to recover.

Even after I was finally able to work again, the world seemed to be pressing in on me. I felt that I hadn't grieved for my father because I'd been too busy. I didn't think I'd done enough for my family. I believed that I was worthless because I couldn't successfully handle everything. The relationship with my fiancé was failing and, of course, I blamed myself.

I was having headaches two or three times a week now. One night I came home and my head was pounding with pain. I couldn't take all the stress anymore. Feeling I couldn't do anything right, I sat on the stairs and cried.

Gekko Applied a Rabbit Remedy

While I cried, something started patting my leg. I looked down to see Gekko sitting on the step next to me with his front paws in my lap. His whiskers quivered with concern.

The last few months hadn't been easy for Gekko either. I was gone often, and many evenings all he got was his dinner and a quick affectionate ear tug. By this time, we'd adopted a second rabbit that Gekko didn't like and fought against. Gekko now had to share me with another human and an additional rabbit. Though I tried very hard to lavish attention on him, it wasn't the amount he'd been accustomed to. And we both knew it.

But now, his concern was evident. When I cried more, he ran up and down the stairs next to me with his ears flopping. He'd stop to pat me with his paws, then dance away, leaping in funny little acrobatics, trying hard to make me laugh. When all else failed, he crawled into my lap and washed my face.

My life began to change that night. I stroked his ears and watched his eyes close in bliss. Then, Gekko licked my chin with the most loving expression I'd ever seen on an animal. I realized that, despite everything, this little rabbit loved me completely. His love made me realize that I had to be worth something and I needed to prove it to myself.

By the end of the summer, I moved out of the apartment I'd shared with my fiancé. With help from my family, I bought a mobile home. Two weeks after I moved I found a different job that paid better, had more favorable hours, and was much less stressful. I broke up with my fiancé, went into counseling, and searched for a treatment to help my migraines.

Through everything, Gekko has been my companion. I have two other rabbits now, and Gekko has made peace with them. Even though they're both darlings, Gekko continues to be a constant source of affection and support. He dances away my sorrow and depression, snuggles with me while I watch movies, and makes me get up in the morning when I'd like nothing more than to hide from the world.

I've finally learned to slow down. I spend my evenings and weekends dancing with rabbits. I've learned to enjoy simple things like planting my indoor garden and embroidery. Most importantly, I've stopped running out of my house. I've turned it into a home that is truly mine, filling it with laughter and joy that was brought into my life by "only a rabbit."

A Foot to Thump: Are you in need of some rabbit relaxation techniques? Could the spiritual lessons from Camille's story remind you to take time to enjoy—and emulate—angel animals who know how to reduce stress and turn houses into homes?

David likes to Rollerblade, bowl, read, draw, golf, and play basketball. He is a thirteen-year-old born-again Christian and is active in his church youth group in Riverview, Michigan. An angel animal, Pookie, taught his family how to offer the special care his sister required.

Pookie Taught Us How to Be Better Caretakers

David Leigh Litwin

We have a wonderful little cat named Pookie who seems to be like a guardian angel. My sister, Amber, has multiple medical problems. During the night when Amber coughs, Pookie comes into her bedroom from wherever he is in the house, even our basement. He then goes into my parents' room and wakes one of them up if they haven't taken care of Amber. When they come into the room, Pookie jumps up onto the beam that crosses above her bed and watches. He won't leave until he knows that Amber is okay. Then he goes back to where he was before.

When Amber was very sick last spring, my mom was at her bedside almost continually for three days. When Mom would have to leave the room, she'd return to find Pookie sitting on her chair keeping watch over my sister.

Maybe there's a reason why Pookie shows so much compassion and gives us more than typical cat behavior.

We didn't raise Pookie from a kitten, but we do know that when he was very tiny, people kept Pookie in a closet. One day when he tried to wander out, his little head got smashed in the door. The people bottle-fed Pookie for three days and didn't think he'd live. They told us that ever since, Pookie had acted as if he were brain-damaged. We said that with all we'd been through due to my sister's condition, including sleep deprivation, we sometimes seemed brain-damaged too!

Since Pookie and Amber are basically nonverbal, they've learned to communicate with each other and us in very creative ways. Having Pookie share our home has helped us to understand Amber better. This cat has shown us that we all give up our secrets, if you take the time to love us enough.

A Paw to Lick: Could Pookie be an angelic messenger sent to help this family learn how to receive the health care Amber needed? Is an angel animal trying to show you how to give a sick or injured person or animal extra vigilance?

Ann is a writer and producer who lives with her husband and business partner, Alden Butcher, in Chanhassen, Minnesota. They have three cats and two dogs and love to take long walks in the woods near their home. Ann's story shows how angel animals protect our lives and spiritual health in miraculous ways.

The Dolphins Saved My Life

ANN ARCHER

It was Christmas vacation, and I went home for the holiday to visit my mother on Hilton Head Island, South Carolina. I loved coming to the island. It renewed my sense of self and restored my health. Here I felt connected to my roots, nature, and the vast oceans. At the time of this visit, on Christmas Day, I had graduated from college and was teaching high school. I loved my work, but it was very demanding physically, emotionally, and mentally. The island was a sanctuary where I felt that the universe might actually hear my call for renewal.

I longed to just dive into the ocean and swim until I could swim no more. I wanted to vent my energies and relax totally. Always a strong swimmer, my family had called me a fish because I taught myself to swim at age two. As a child, I'd swim long distances, staying in the water all day and loving every minute.

Around noon on this holiday, I went to the beach and walked alone on the warm sands along the water's edge. The sun was brilliant, but most people sitting on the beach probably thought that the water was too cool for swimming. Vacationers on this international island resort greeted me with a variety of accents as I gathered shells.

When I felt warm enough, I walked into the ocean waves and dove in. I swam hard and fast. Even when I felt tired, I continued. At last I rolled over on my back and looked toward the beach. I was amazed to be so far away from the shore. The people on the beach were tiny specks and a large expanse of ocean waves separated us.

This had been my family home for years, so I knew these waters well. My mind raced to warnings I'd received. The few sharks that had ever been sighted in this area were known to be attracted to shrimp boats, but none were in sight. Even though no one else was in the water, I didn't feel frightened.

I began my long swim back with strong strokes. I loved the smell of the fresh salt air. The water's temperature had become comfortable. I swam in total abandon until I again checked the shoreline. It was as if I'd barely moved. I could feel myself being pulled out to sea. Trying not to panic, I reminded myself that people watching me from the shore had probably seen how far I'd gone out.

A Dark Fin Appeared

Suddenly I was frozen with fear because off to my left a dark fin moved directly toward me. My heart pounded wildly. I stopped swimming and attempted to float and bob in the water, stretched out like a log on the surface. I could barely breath. I closed my eyes. I tried desperately to keep my mind from entertaining the horrors of being eaten by a shark. Suddenly, a powerful, smooth, sleek body rose underneath me.

I couldn't imagine what was happening. I felt my body being lifted slightly. While gliding across the water's surface, I was being moved toward the shore. Then slowly, gently, I was lowered back into the ocean. I instantly felt the strange sensation of a powerful body rising up, then lifting and carrying me forward.

The surface of the water broke in front of me and I could finally see the creature who was carrying me. It was a beautiful dolphin who jumped through the air, looked at me, dived to the left, and dipped underwater again. All the while, I moved through the water at great speed while another of these wonderful animals appeared. Soon, I was surrounded by a school of dolphins circling me. One at a time they moved beneath me, lifting and carrying me back to shore as if they were performing an orchestrated dance or choreographed ballet.

A Special Christmas Day Show

The dolphins took turns carrying me, then leaping in front and moving around. One to the left. One to the right. Quickly and smoothly, they brought me to chest-high water. Then they encircled me, spinning, diving, smiling. The dolphins called in an amazing, high-pitched language that filled me with delight. I clapped in appreciation for the show they were providing. Touched and in awe, I couldn't stop talking to and thanking them. Eventually they turned, said farewell, and danced out to sea.

By this time, a crowd of people had gathered on the shore.

They'd seen the dark fin and anticipated a shark attack. After watching my incredible return to shore on the backs of frolicking dolphins, they greeted me, laughing, talking, and questioning about how the dolphins rescued me. What a memorable moment! Communicating with people from all over the world who had somehow come together to witness something none of us would ever forget. It was a marvelous gift on this special Christmas Day.

The dolphins helped me relate to the blessings of nature, as I had never before. I became more aware that all life is connected by a divine thread of love. Totally renewed in spirit, I felt confident that the universe supports me.

A Wave to Ride: A friend told us that in the U.S. Navy during World War II, many stories circulated about dolphins who saved sailors from drowning after their ships wrecked. The dolphins would carry the men back to shore and safety.

Is an angel animal renewing and restoring your own health and well-being? Could we learn from angel animals about giving each other boosts? Is there someone in your life who has hit choppy waters or floated too far out and needs a ride on your back to make it to shore?

Anthony is from Ridgecrest, California. He is retired from the U.S. Navy and U.S. civil service. His two cats, Mocha and Fraidy, share his home. Anthony says he loves cats and has "lots and lots of paw prints" on his heart. He tells the story of a special cat's compassion for one who thought life had no more to offer.

A Needy Cat Offered Me a Reason to Live

Anthony Taylor

When D.C. came into my life I'd just about reached the bottom of a long trip through the depths of alcoholism and was on the verge of losing everything I had, including my family. Those nearest and dearest to me still held on to a spark of love, but even they didn't want to be with me for more than a few minutes at a time. My emotional state had deteriorated to the point that I'd already decided I didn't want to go on living. I was desperately trying to drink myself to death. Feeling that there was no purpose to my life, I was approaching the time when I would have nerve enough to take more effective steps to end it.

One day, in a stupor, I stumbled to the back door and looked to see what it was like outside. I spotted a little skinny kitten in the neighbor's yard. He looked up at me and somehow knew, without question, that he'd found a cat person. You can change that to *sucker* if you want, because I've always been a real sucker for cats. I think that one quick glance across the yard cemented our relationship. The cat didn't hesitate an instant, didn't even wait to be called, just came running and jumped over the fence. He bounded up the steps and planted himself against my leg, as if staking his claim. I didn't know it then, but this cat would remain pretty close to that leg for the next fifteen years.

For a few weeks, neither of us acknowledged that he'd become my cat. He was supposed to belong to our neighbors. They probably thought the kitten still belonged to them, but I already had his heart and unflagging loyalty. When I met D.C., we were both rejects on our way to being booted out. We were to form a very special kinship.

How D.C. Got His Name

It was really something to see D.C. come running from under the neighbor's house when I'd bang my screen door. The sound alerted him that his new buddy was up and around and the food dish would shortly be brimming with goodies. He also knew he'd get lots of patting and rubbing before being allowed to sleep in a nice, soft bed instead of on the dirt under a mobile home.

When I first met the little orange kitten, it seemed as if he could never get enough to eat. His face was always down in the food dish, and every time he came up for air his chin was dirty, because he really burrowed in. He wasn't my cat then, so I didn't give him a name right away. Instead, I called him Dirty-Chin, Little Old Cat. That was quite a mouthful and eventually my daughters suggested it would be easier to just name him D.C., short for Dirty Chin. After we completed the process of stealing D.C. a little more each day from our neighbors, who moved away without taking him with them, we put D.C. on his medical records and that officially became his name.

D.C. Loved Me During My Time of Despair

D.C. wasn't afraid of me at all and after a good meal he'd follow me back into my bedroom where I spent more and more time in my own foggy world of misery and despair. He didn't seem to mind the smell of unwashed human or spilled beer and bourbon. Instead he'd jump up on my chest and thoroughly clean my beard with his tongue, going at the task with a purpose. In those moments, I felt a strong bond growing and knew that of all the cats I'd loved, this one was going to be very important to me.

Once D.C. was missing for eight long days. I knew he wouldn't voluntarily leave and I expected the worst. I was one very miserable person without my pal. Scouring the neighborhood, I desperately feared finding his lifeless body. He eventually showed up, tired and very dirty. He acted as if he'd been out for a casual stroll, but his paws told a different story. The pads on his feet were almost worn off, indicating that his journey home had been a long one. Apparently, someone had taken him away, but my buddy managed to find his way home. The hungry little fellow really buried his chin in the food dish that time.

D.C. Saved My Life

My sickness progressed to the point that I finally decided to take my own life. Just about the time I was preparing to do the deed, D.C. came in and said, "Cut out whatever you're doing and come feed me." You might be skeptical that the cat was actually talking to me. If so, you just don't know how strong the bond was between us. Or you don't know drunks very well. D.C. and I talked to each other a lot.

I stopped what I was doing and went into the kitchen to feed him. I might have been planning to end it all, but I had my priorities straight. When this cat was hungry, he had to be fed. Somehow, D.C. had sidetracked me from my mission long enough for me to realize two things. First, I wasn't in any condition to make such a serious decision as ending my life. And second, at least one of God's creatures might miss me if I wasn't around.

I began to think that maybe there was a purpose for my life, even if was just to feed that little orange cat.

My alcoholism worsened until I finally got sick enough to call for help. I went into an alcohol rehabilitation treatment center. There, I came to realize that D.C. had come to me when we needed each other. He'd needed me to open a door and take him in. I needed him to open a heart and let me in.

For reasons I don't understand I couldn't hear the humans who had tried to help me. But I heard D.C. loudly and clearly. Why he was able to stir the remaining spark of humanity in me is a mystery. I just knew that as long as D.C. sat on my lap I felt good. If I wanted to have him back there, I knew that I must successfully complete my treatment. I had to live.

With a new purpose, I finished the program and have been sober ever since.

D.C. Left His Legacy

Old age and past injuries finally brought the little cat down. D.C. had arthritis, which caused bone spurs to develop so that walking was very painful. He couldn't see much anymore, and although we still called him our guard cat, he'd quit climbing to the top of the car to do his tour of duty. He'd settled for sitting on the back stoop and watching for intruders. He no longer went with me when I walked the few yards down to my mother's house, where he had a special place on his very own footstool. When I returned from those visits, he couldn't bound up the street to meet me because he didn't recognize me until I was close. And he simply no longer bounded.

D.C. still demanded his place on my lap even though the pain of getting up and down must have been terrible. I'd try to talk him out of it, telling him that he could stay beside my feet, but he'd have no part of that. He'd scratch my knee and look at me with pleading eyes until I lifted him up. He'd cry out, and when the pain was exceptionally severe, as an automatic reflex, he'd bite me. He'd apologize for the unintentional bite by licking my chin until it nearly bled. He didn't need to apologize. I knew the end was near and I even cherished his bites.

Maybe it had just been my imagination all those years when I swear the cat talked to me, because when I really needed him to speak, he didn't. He'd sit on my lap and stare into my eyes. I desperately wanted him to tell me it was okay to do what I felt must be done. I hope I heard him correctly, because I couldn't stand to see the pain in his eyes anymore and we knew we had to end his suffering with euthanasia.

I relied on my twelve-step program. I prayed to God to show me what to do and to give me the strength to do it. Somehow, I made the decision, but I couldn't take that long, last trip to the vet's office. My wife took care of the awful job. I'll always be grateful to her for making such a sacrifice.

In Celebration of D.C.'s Life

I have no doubt that D.C. saved my life. He gave me something to live for when I didn't think I had anything. Because of those extra years, I developed a real friendship with my wife, even though I'd nearly driven her out of her wits. Because of D.C., I lived to know and desperately love my wonderful grandchildren.

Today, I have completed a successful career. I've turned into a much better person than I was before D.C. and I met. I could write a whole book about the wonderful times D.C. and I shared and the things I gained because of him.

Since D.C. gave me a reason to live, I had to write this story to celebrate his life. Having his name in print for others to see acknowledges that D.C. was Somebody with a capital S. Because he existed, I lived to sit at a keyboard and write about my pal. About how he made a human being out of me. About how I tried to make one out of him.

I think we each came pretty close.

> **A Paw to Lick:** The image of D.C. licking Anthony's beard and giving him a reason to live demonstrates the miraculous healing powers of an angel animal's unconditional love. Is there someone—an animal or a human—who is too hard for you to love? Can D.C.'s example help you find some way to reach out and help a tortured creature to heal?

You met Kristy and her cats Misha and Bani, in chapter 3. She's an ordained minister, jogger, cyclist, gardener, and researcher who teaches nutrition classes for children and adults. Kristy shares her home with cats Misha and Isabella and three saltwater fish. This story reminds us that angel animals can show us how to trust our own truth.

Feeling Bad? Consult a Cat

Kristy Walker

Misha, my very intuitive and sensitive Siamese cat, often shows me God's love in moments when I'm feeling sad. Misha seems to have the ability to know when I need extra love.

He also seems to know exactly what he needs.

Once Misha had an eye infection. I'd taken him to the vet and asked for herbal medicine. However, Misha didn't seem to like this prescription. He wouldn't let me put it in his eye. So, I asked the vet for another type of medicine. I wanted to get something that might heal Misha's eye faster because I was going out of town. The vet gave me a cortisone cream.

Well, Misha didn't like this medication either. I went to get the cream to give him a treatment but I couldn't find the tube anywhere. When I found it, I discovered that Misha had bitten holes all over the tube. If I squeezed it, the medicine spurted out everywhere. When I saw what Misha had done, I remembered how intuitive he is and thought, *Maybe Misha is trying to tell me something about this medicine.*

Misha Knew Best

I took Misha back to the vet and asked if we needed to do something different to heal his eye infection. After she examined him, the vet said, "Yes, we do." She said that none of her patients had ever told her so explicitly that the medication needed to be changed.

Misha is a very smart cat and I pay attention when he doesn't act like himself. I know that Misha is more than a cat. He's a soul who communicates with me if I listen. I knew that he wouldn't bite into that tube of medicine just for the fun of it. The vet and I just had to figure out what Misha already knew in his own heart about what was best for his health.

A Paw to Lick: Should we be paying more attention when angel animals try to communicate with us about their health? If a Siamese cat knows when something isn't right for him, do we also have an inner awareness of how to be healthier?

More Healthy Living

In a program called pet- or animal-assisted therapy, dogs, cats, rabbits, or other small domesticated animals visit children's hospitals, AIDS and cancer wards, and nursing homes. Angel animals minister to the sick, lonely, and abused.

The Puppy and the Paralyzed Man

Linda volunteers to take animals from a local humane society to a center for the disabled in Minneapolis. She says, "I took a fourteen-week-old boxer-mix puppy for one visit. She was very shy, but the volunteer coordinator assured me that the pup would be fine. This puppy turned out to be a wonderful, natural healer! She cuddled with everyone as I placed her on the laps of each person in a wheelchair. I was touched to watch as a blind woman smiled broadly while stroking the puppy's soft fur.

After the puppy visited with everyone, I asked a staff person if I should place the dog with a man who appeared to be completely paralyzed. I sensed that, although he couldn't speak, this stroke victim had been aware of the puppy's presence. When the coordinator asked the man if he wanted the puppy on his chest, he blinked. This was his way of saying, "Yes." The right eyelid was the only part of his body that he could move. I put the puppy against the man's heart, and she licked his chin. Then the coordinator asked the man if he liked the puppy. He blinked his right eyelid again. On the way back to the shelter, I thanked the puppy profusely for all the love she'd given to these people who needed her kisses.

In the next chapter, you're going to meet angel animals who show us how to surrender to the love that is within life, to trust that we're all in God's tender hands.

Chapter Seven

Letting Go and Trusting

The dove on the branch giving thanks. The glorious singing of the nightingales. The gnat. The elephant. Every living thing trusts in God for its nourishment.

—Jelaluddin Rumi, from "A Man and Woman Arguing"

At the animal shelter where Linda volunteers, the older dogs are often dazed, confused, and mistrustful. The reasons humans have given for leaving them include moving, divorce, new baby, allergies—excuses that maybe aren't so great from the viewpoint of animals who have given love, loyalty, and friendship for years.

Linda has learned that the dogs need someone to understand their distress. So she communicates with them in an attempt to comfort the animals. First, she gets a dog's attention with hugging or by playing with him. Then she places an image in her mind while speaking to the dog. Linda will know by the attentive look on the dog's face that the animal is now listening intently.

Animals pick up images and sense the love Linda sends to them telepathically. Then they return their own images to "answer" her. Linda has to trust what she's receiving, which is not an easy thing to do, because humans usually only accept what they hear physically—not this kind of heart-to-heart interspecies "talking."

Communicating Doggie Adoption Tips

When Linda walks the dogs at the shelter, sometimes she asks them, "Do you want to know something that might help you find a new home?" If the dogs are willing, she'll tell them what she's observed. To some dogs she's said, "You're barking too much." She told one dog that he was jumping too high and scaring people. Then she noticed that every time she passed his cage, the dog, who before their "conversation" had looked as if he were wired to a pogo stick, would bounce up only a little when he saw her pass by. He was trying.

Linda told one little pup that if she wanted to go to a new home, she'd have to pay more attention to the humans and less to the other dogs. The dog walked away from Linda and ignored her. Then she flashed an image that came through loudly and clearly. She said, "I don't want to go home with a human. Humans hurt you." Linda immediately hugged the dog and said, "Not all humans hurt. Someone is going to love you very much."

A dog named Brandy seemed not to be very interested in hearing the advice "To get love, you're going to have to give some." But when Linda returned him to the kennel after their walk, Brandy acted like a new dog. He walked calmly and didn't pull on the leash. As Linda prepared to leave, she overheard two women commenting on the sign with a photo of Brandy as "Pet of the Week." They planned to visit him. Linda flashed Brandy a quick message, "Here's your chance!" The next time Linda volunteered, she was thrilled to find that all the dogs she'd "talked" with had been adopted.

Since more than 90 percent of all human communication is nonverbal, maybe it's not so surprising that animals and humans can speak to each other in the language of the heart without so many words. In this chapter, you're going to read about angel animals who are teaching humans some new tricks besides how to talk to them. They're showing us how to trust ourselves, to trust life, to trust God.

JoAnn says that she's sought the "meaning of life" for many years. She lives in Lexington, Kentucky, where she works as a travel agent. She's also a writer and a painter. JoAnn believes that life is good when its purpose is to help people by discovering their special talents. In this story she recalls an encounter with an angel animal who helped her trust again that God loves her.

Kuro Crossed the River of Hope

JoAnn M. Quintos

My mom and I went to Japan when I was seven years old because my Japanese grandfather was dying. It was strange to be in a country that was half my heritage. When I arrived, my Japanese language skills were poor, but they developed rapidly.

I became close friends with two of my cousins. Their innocence and wonder at life uplifted me. At the age of only seven, I was very jaded. I'd been through the divorce of my parents. I'd been molested. I was anything but innocent!

My cousins and I adopted a stray black, furry dog. We named him Kuro, which is Japanese for black. He was a little mutt, but we loved him so much.

Once there was a torrential rainstorm. My grandfather's house was next to a normally peaceful, quiet river. Two days of rain raised the water level so that the river resembled rapids in Colorado. During this deluge, Kuro disappeared. My cousins and I would go outside screaming, "Kuro!" and return drenched and disheartened. Our parents scolded us for venturing out in the storms and rain.

The weird thing was that we could hear Kuro crying and

whimpering from across the river when we called him. But we couldn't see him anywhere.

On the second day of the rains, we stood at the banks of the river and called and called. Kuro answered with pathetic cries. My cousins told me that we'd better go back inside. I told them to go on without me, that I'd be there shortly.

After my cousins left, I prayed as I'd never prayed before. I didn't know if I should pray in English or in Japanese! My over-riding thought was of how much that little dog meant to me, and I focused all my love on him.

When I opened my eyes, I saw Kuro walking out of the water. This was impossible. The river was too wide, and the rapids too powerful for a little dog to swim.

At this bad time in my life, my faith in God and my hope were replenished by Kuro's return. I realized that in my time of need, with the power of love, miracles can happen.

A Tail to Wag: Have you gone through experiences that have taught you not to trust that you're loved? Could an angel animal be trying to deliver the message—across a raging river of doubt and pain—that you are loved, cherished, and protected by a higher power?

Victoria enjoys travel, song writing, swimming, and feeding raccoons at her home in Tiburon, California. Since the age of twelve, she has been doing volunteer work in the areas of literacy, the homeless, and abused animals. Victoria is a writer who has been a guest on many radio shows. Her amazing story about a special angel animal cat who assists in healing others inspires all of us to trust the loving creatures who are here to help us.

The Cat Who Knew How to Let Go of Pain

Victoria Bullis

I've been working for a long time now on an unusual project. With the help of a special cat named Homer, I learned how to teach animals to be little healers for other animals and humans. Here's how it all began.

About a dozen years ago, a client of mine named Lydia asked if I could help a cat she had rescued from some teenage bullies. This cat had been severely tortured and was in a state of shock. I felt immediately that I could help him and suggested that she bring him to me the next morning.

Even though she described how this poor creature, whose name was Homer, looked after his traumatic experience, I wasn't prepared for what I saw. Tears welled up in my eyes when I saw the little fellow. It was impossible to tell what breed he was because his fur had been entirely burned away, except for one patch of gray at the top of his head. It looked as though he'd probably lose sight in one of his eyes. Understandably, this cat was terrified of everything around him, even his rescuer.

When Homer arrived at my office, he was lying on an old army blanket in a slatted wooden orange crate. Lydia set the carton on the floor next to me. The scrawny kitty whimpered and shook convulsively, cowering in the far corner. He needed time to adjust to me, so I waited before attempting to touch him or pick him up. I gestured with hand movements, to indicate that Lydia and I should sit quietly.

I Tried to Communicate with Homer

I closed my eyes and tried to communicate telepathically with Homer. Suddenly, I had the inspiration to ask for angelic support. My prayers must have been answered, because Homer calmed down a bit. When he appeared to be more peaceful, I carefully placed a catnip toy at the other end of the crate and put a little plate of steamed salmon in there for him. He didn't move for a few more moments, so I began talking softly to him. Immediately, he got a crazed look in his eyes and hissed at me.

I switched back to communicating with him telepathically and noticed that his breathing became more regular. The wild look in his eyes diminished. I waited quite a while until I spoke again. The results were the same as the first time. He seemed traumatized by hearing a human voice.

I decided to try another healing technique on this severely injured animal. In my imagination, I surrounded him with soft, healing colors. When I realized this and a few other techniques I tried also weren't working, I became discouraged. It looked as if I wouldn't be able to reach him at all that day.

As I was about to tell Lydia that we should try to help him another time, Homer slowly reached out a little blistered paw and took one bat at the catnip mouse. Lydia and I glanced at each other out of the corners of our eyes and watched as he pawed lethargically at the cloth toy for about a quarter of an hour. I telepathically encouraged him to take a bite of fish. He hadn't eaten anything for the three days that he'd been with Lydia.

After what seemed like hours, Homer started to drag himself, inch by minuscule inch, on his belly, toward the plate. He reached out and speared a tiny flake of salmon, sniffing it tentatively for a moment, and licking it off his paw. Then he placed the salmon on his tongue and sneezed! This startled us into moving involuntarily, and we were afraid that we'd ruined the mood. Instead, our movement seemed to be a catalyst for shifting Homer into feeling safer with us. He took even larger bites off the plate, until he'd eaten the entire fillet. I remember wishing I'd bought a larger piece, because he might have eaten more, as hungry as he must have been.

I didn't try to touch him that day nor during any of the next several visits. Since Homer seemed to respond best to telepathy, I used that method to let him know how much I loved him and to assure him that he was beautiful. I told him I thought it was important that he lived. Every so often I'd speak aloud to get him used to my voice. I'd say how much better he looked than the last time we'd visited.

In between our sessions, I telepathically sent my little patient healing messages, which he began to accept and eventually seemed to eagerly await. I taught Lydia how to talk to him this way— through the heart instead of the voice. Homer began to improve dramatically. His fur grew back in clumps and he ate voraciously. He finally stopped having a nervous twitch. He responded with increasing playfulness to toys Lydia gave him.

Homer Communicated with Me

After three months of slow but steady improvement, I mentioned to Lydia that Homer probably didn't need my help anymore, and told her that this could be our last appointment. As soon as I said these things to Lydia, Homer, who had been lying on her lap, mewed, jumped down, and walked agitatedly around my office. I tried to understand his behavior.

Then I received a clear, strong telepathic message from the cat saying that he'd been sending information to me for some time and I wasn't getting it. Surprised, I replied that I was sorry, and asked him what he wanted me to know.

Homer said that many other animals are ill and suffering. This cat, who'd been through so much pain himself, then told me that he wanted to do for other animals what I'd done for him. He flashed a series of images to me about how to help him achieve his goal of helping others. I excitedly transmitted that I'd love working with him in this unique way.

Homer purred for the first time since I'd met him.

Lydia was intrigued with the concept and agreed to experiment with it. I called someone I knew at my local Society for the Prevention of Cruelty to Animals (SPCA) and asked if he'd like to join me in fulfilling Homer's wish to help other animals. I asked the man to describe any animal and tell me the reason he or she had come to the shelter. I said that I'd convey this information to my "student," Homer, to see if we could help.

The man from the SPCA agreed to participate. He described a dog who had been in the shelter for over a week. I passed on the information to Homer that we were now working with a despondent and lonely Doberman. I showed Homer how to psychically connect with the dog and allow healing energy to flow through him to benefit the other animal. Homer immediately understood. He even added his own empathic message. I could sense the big animal at the shelter perking up and feeling some hope. I called my cohort at the shelter to see if the depressed Doberman had reacted to Homer's assistance. He was astonished at the immediate change of expression on the dog's face. He offered to assist with Homer's work on a regular basis.

Six months later, Homer had the opportunity to use his healing service with a human. A woman with newly detected Hodgkin's disease made an appointment to see me. As soon as she sat down I felt Homer with me, letting me know he wanted to help her. I heard him say telepathically to the despairing woman that she was a wonderful person and deserved to live!

From then on, throughout the remainder of his life, every time

I worked with someone who had physical or emotional challenges, I'd feel Homer with us spiritually, passing on loving and
energizing messages. As if to offer proof that Homer, the healing
cat, was really assisting, more than a few of these people later
mentioned that they'd begun to dream about cats or that they'd
decided to adopt one!

Homer Inspired Me to Teach Other Animals

After Homer and I fine-tuned our connection, I knew that I
wanted to work with other types of animals too. First, I experi-
mented with pets of people I knew to enlist their help in healing
others. Word soon spread of my work with animals, and soon a
few dog trainers and a veterinarian called to enlist my services.

After the many years of helping to develop the healing capacities between animals and humans, what has amazed me the most
is how comfortable people are with the concept. I believe we
must be remembering a connection we all had with animals in
ancient times, one in which we communicated easily and trusted
one another for help through the pain and suffering of our lives.

A Paw to Lick: When you pray for help or healing, would you
like to add the words "Thy will be done" to remember that God
will do what's best in any situation? Could Homer's example inspire you to turn pain and suffering into a catalyst for giving
love and service?

Wayne, who you met in chapter 2, is from Anstead, Australia. His family of pets includes two dogs, three cats, magpies, kookaburras, koalas, possums, and wallabies who roam the Australian bush near his home. Wayne says that the animals teach him the fundamentals of nature with their astounding revelations and antics. Wayne's story shows that an angel animal in the wild, who is treated with love and respect, can display heartwarming trust and gratitude.

A Koala and I Trusted Each Other

WAYNE HUDSON

Our small acreage forms part of one of the largest koala corridors in Australia. Each year, especially during the mating season, a number of these endearing creatures pass through our property. Due to the encroachment of suburbia, the koalas suffer from stress and its consequences. The threat of dogs, traffic, and fences decrease their resistance and make them more susceptible to a contagious disease that causes blindness, cystitis, and infertility.

As I was leaving home one day, I noticed a distressed koala walking around in circles. When our neighbors came home, they helped my family secure the animal. Attempts to confine him looked like a surreal dance with humans chasing a koala and a koala chasing humans. Capturing a koala is never easy, because they have powerful, sharp claws. Since this one was nearly blind, each human was a potential tree to climb.

After we caught the koala, we contacted the wildlife authorities who operate on and nurse these animals back to health. The officers and volunteers perform miracles rehabilitating sick and injured animals and returning them to the wild.

The Koala Was Free to Leave

Two weeks after the initial contact, the wildlife ranger said that the koala was ready to be returned to his familiar territory. The ranger placed a cage with the animal in it at the base of a large eucalyptus tree and opened the door. Usually, a koala released in this manner will dash out and rapidly climb the nearest tree. But not this one. Instead of running away, he looked directly at me with his clear, doelike eyes. I stood transfixed in his gaze.

I'm sure he's saying, "Thank you," I thought. The ranger reached out and scratched the koala's back. I watched as the koala climbed the tree slowly until he reached a safe height. Still, he didn't leave, but stayed near our home for a number of days, bringing great delight and joy to my family and friends. The koala became such a familiar friend that we named him Sebastian.

It seemed to me that this whole episode was an exercise in which people and animals learned to trust one another. We were given a special opportunity to compensate for encroaching on the koala's territory by helping him get well. And, by staying nearby and letting us get to know him better, the animal expressed his gratitude by giving us the chance to commune with wildlife.

A Tree to Climb: Is someone you know being displaced by having to let go of familiar places and things? What could you do to let others know that you're a friend to be relied on when they're feeling invaded and threatened?

Ilona is a writer and inspirational speaker from Minneapolis, Minnesota. She works as an archivist and is a minister in her church. She and her husband, Jon, compose and produce music through their company, Eagle Wings Productions. They enjoy rabbits, pheasants, and other wildlife that visit their garden, and look forward to soon adding a miniature poodle to their family. Ilona's story serves as a primer for how to communicate with and gain the trust of an angel animal.

A Conversation with the Brokenhearted Horse

ILONA GOIN

Horses are at the heart of my first memories of animals. Growing up in a city, I had few opportunities to be around horses, but they fascinated me. On the rare occasions when I met one, I'd gleefully run to commune with him. Even the humblest horse seemed glorious to me.

These regal, intelligent creatures gave me peace and joy; their watchful silence and calm demeanor comforted me. Even as a toddler, I wasn't concerned about their imposing size. I sensed that, if frightened, these gentle herbivores would rather flee than fight.

Because I admired horses so much, I yearned to communicate with them. Intuitively, I knew that interspecies communication was possible. It was up to me to find the key to making it happen.

I Met a Horse I Could Talk To

One fall afternoon, when I lived in a Seattle suburb during the mid-1980s, I had an experience that changed my relationship with all animals. It not only provided the key but also unlocked the door to my having the deep interaction with animals I'd longed for since childhood. My first conversation with a horse brought a new understanding of human nature and how inter-dependent all creatures are.

Next to a house, I saw a horse who occupied a rectangular pen that was too small for even the one animal who lived there. The owners had simply fenced in their backyard, and the lawn had long since deteriorated under the forces of muzzle and hooves. All that remained was a patch of black soil marred by hoof prints, devoid of even the smallest tuft of grass or weed.

Horses are flight animals, created by nature to outrun their predators and to cover miles each day in search of food. Not soli-tary animals, horses depend on their herd for survival.

Yet, before me stood a lone, dark brown gelding, surrounded by tall trees that cast shadows across his little patch of earth. Robbed of everything that gives horses a sense of safety, dignity, and happiness, he looked like a cornered animal that had lost his will to live.

I was appalled that these conditions were considered to be a property owner's right rather than mistreatment. I empathized deeply with the poor creature. I moved closer to him, away from my car, as if to distance myself from the human race. I felt embar-rassed to be lumped in with those who would treat an intelligent, sensitive being so callously. I wanted to apologize and explain that not all people are as unaware as those who had imprisoned him. But most of all, that day, I wanted to view life from his perspective.

I Learned the Horse's Language

I stood still, facing the gelding, and wondered how he experienced life. He appeared rooted to the middle of his pen, his left side toward me, head hung low as if he were pretending to nibble on phantom grass. "Look, I'm a harmless grazer," he seemed to say. In horse language, he was telling me that he wasn't worried about my presence, nor did he pose a threat to me. In fact, the bend of his head showed a degree of submissiveness that bordered on depression. If I shifted my weight a little, he'd rotate one ear and focus his left eye on me for a moment. Then he'd resume his withdrawn state.

I wanted the horse to know that there was much more to life than he'd been allowed to experience. But my human thoughts and feelings, even my empathy, brought no response from him. I realized that if this animal was ever going to know how I felt, I had to stop thinking. If I wanted him to hear and trust me, I must understand what he was listening for. He couldn't meet me on my level, so I had to find his. And to tune in to this creature's wavelength, I'd have to become like a horse.

My attention began to slide up and down the spectrum of consciousness. I attempted to move beyond thought, even beyond emotions and images, to a state of pure perception. It was a little like turning the tuning knob on the radio in search of a particular station. When I found the right one, I recognized it instantly. But this was a two-way radio—the horse could hear me, and I could hear him.

The gelding raised his head and looked at me with interest. His ears pointed forward, as if listening to an outer signal. I sent an impression along this frequency. In human terms, the message was, "I hear you. I'm friendly. Greetings."

I Interviewed the Horse

I wasn't sure what to expect, but the wave that returned astonished me. It contained a myriad of impressions, all transmitted in an instant. Then a series of waves began to flow back and forth between us, consisting of something like an interview. I posed "questions," then listened to the gelding's responses. Unlike a human conversation, the interaction consisted of a series of insights. Rather than take turns expressing ideas, as people do, we seemed to share our state of consciousness through a type of telepathic link. The form and content of the communication opened me to a new understanding of consciousness.

When we began our "conversation," the horse was skeptical about my intentions. A human who whispered horse language was as new to him as it was to me. He had every right to be suspicious. Despite my communication skills, after all, I was still a human, and he'd learned to distrust all of my species. Why should he believe I'd be any different from those who had hurt him?

I already knew that animals experience many feelings and the more evolved species have thought processes. But I'd never imagined the depth and nuances of a horse's inner life. This horse was not merely bored, he was despondent, and his mood was as black as the barren earth beneath him.

Too depressed to be angry, he had no feelings beyond disdain and bitterness. Humans had repeatedly disappointed him. He had given up hope.

He Wouldn't Believe Me

I tried to tell the horse that there is love in the world, but he wouldn't believe it. His own experiences had taught him otherwise. Just as humans do when they're too wounded to take another chance on life, he rejected my encouragement. I wanted him to know that many humans are more aware and caring. This didn't matter to him. As many traumatized humans do, he stubbornly clung to his convictions about the lot of us.

Trying to communicate with this horse reinforced my understanding of the relationship between animals and humans. I believe that no one can degrade or limit another individual without doing the same to himself. As we hang the rope of domination around another creature's neck, we also bind ourselves. After all, we are holding the other end.

I remembered that I was merely a guest in the horse's realm. The gelding was in charge of this interview. Soon, he got bored with the whole thing and dropped his head back to that sad, familiar position. Our conversation was clearly ending. To express my thanks and to "sign off," I began to pray softly and gently, in a way that I've found is spiritually uplifting for people and soothing to animals.

Did a Guardian Angel for Horses Appear?

Suddenly, the gelding lifted his head high. His eyes and ears focused intently, but not on me; he was looking at a point three or four feet to my left. Simultaneously, I felt the electric presence and intelligence of an invisible spiritual being, a guardian angel, beside me. A cautious glance through the corner of my eye provided no clues about the visitor. Although I couldn't see him, the horse clearly did. I continued to pray as I watched the horse, frozen in his alert position.

The visitor was here for the horse's benefit more than mine, but I was learning my own lessons. His sacred presence exuded benevolence and an aura of love and tranquillity. I was left with a quiet, deep feeling of joy and awe. Judging from the gelding's rapt attention and fearless interest, I had no doubt that our friend made a similar impression on him. Perhaps he was the guardian angel of horses, who had come to show the gelding that he could trust what I'd told him, and to assure the horse that he wasn't alone, but was loved and protected.

As quickly as it arrived, the electric presence disappeared, and the horse once again lowered his head until his muzzle hovered inches from the soil. I drew a deep breath, letting it out slowly while murmuring a silent word of thanks for this remarkable gift. The horse remained impassive. When I returned to my car, I checked my watch, wondering how late I was for the meeting I'd been on my way to attend. To my surprise, the whole experience had lasted only three minutes!

I pondered the windows in time and space that allow us to experience and learn more in a minute than we normally do in a day or more. "What makes these windows suddenly open?" I asked myself. The answer came in one word like a warm wave: love. When we give and receive unconditional love, a window opens into a larger world, bringing greater understanding. Love allows us to travel from point to point throughout the web of life to experience any state of consciousness—even that of a horse.

A Tail to Swish: Could you communicate with angel animals by asking a guardian angel or the Holy Spirit to help you see life from their point of view? Is there an angel animal who needs you to help him trust that there are humans who love and treat animals with respect?

Donald, a retired U.S. Air Force tech sergeant from Elk Grove, California, has been married for forty years and raised a family of four children. Among his many interests are painting, reading, writing, clay sculpture, wood and stone carving, and building houses. Don helps us realize that angel animals, or insects, can also learn to trust humans.

The Grateful Wasp

DONALD D. REYNOLDS

One spring day a tiny black wasp became trapped in our kitchen window. My wife tried to guide him out the open door, but the wasp kept frantically buzzing along the surface of the window. He tried to escape but only grew more frightened at my wife's efforts to help him.

I'd recently read a book in which the author claimed that herd animals were highly telepathic. I thought, *The wasp is a herd animal and so am I. Maybe I can communicate with him.*

I grabbed a straight ruler and placed one end near the buzzing wasp. Then I began my running commentary. I told the wasp, "I'm trying to help you. I know what's wrong and you don't. Trust me and I'll take you out. Just get on the end of this stick."

Immediately, the wasp stopped searching for a way out and climbed onto the end of the ruler. Calmly gripping it, he vibrated his wings. I moved the ruler away from the window and carried the wasp to the door, all the while continuing my reassuring words. I said, "Everything is all right. Trust me. There are forces here that you don't understand, but I do."

Slowly, I carried the wasp to the door. I didn't want him to fly back into the house, so I told him not to run off too soon. I suggested that the wasp wait until I told him to fly.

When I extended my arm and the ruler far out the door into the sunshine, I said to the little wasp, "Everything is okay. You can fly now." And the wasp immediately flew away. I was elated.

A Second Chance at Trust

A few days later, another tiny black wasp, which could have been the little fellow who had visited me and my wife earlier, was caught in the same window. So, I went through the identical procedure with the ruler and clear instructions. Again, the wasp followed my directions, except for one thing. This time, when I told him that it was all right to fly away, instead of sailing off into the wild blue yonder, he landed on the porch railing only a few feet away. Then he turned around very deliberately, looked at me for a few seconds, turned again, and flew off.

I had the distinct impression that the wasp had expressed his gratitude for my help and that this had been his way of saying, "Thank you."

I consider myself to be a spiritual but not a religious man. I'm convinced that so-called spiritual or miraculous experiences are a normal part of everyday life. I believe that communication between the wasp and me seems amazing only because I'd never been taught that different species' lives are connected. Now I've experienced the fact that we aren't separate from each other.

Wings to Fly: Are insects more aware than we've discovered so far? Could you find ways to help humans, animals, or even insects learn to trust by having their best interests at heart when you try to communicate with them?

Trusting the Way Love Communicates

In this chapter you've been reading about angel animals who show us how to take the next steps toward trusting. In "Dillinger Teaches Me to Trust Again," Donna M. Lengyel introduces us to an exceptional angel animal. Donna, a homemaker, mother, and part-time bartender from Tobyhanna, Pennsylvania, writes about a dog who helped her let go of past pain.

Donna adopted Dillinger, a three-legged dog who had been severely abused. She says that she was moved by the beauty and sweetness on this dog's face. Since Donna herself had been abused in a previous relationship, she related to the dog's suffering. She'd been having a hard time trusting her new husband, whom she describes as "the nicest guy in the world," but who "hadn't been able to penetrate the emotional walls I'd built to protect myself."

Over the months Dillinger and Donna learned to communicate with each other. Donna says, "I started talking to him and expressing how mean I knew people can be. Even though I was carrying on one-sided conversations, the interest on Dillinger's face assured me that he knew exactly what I was saying." Donna watched Dillinger trusting a human after what humans had done to him. She says, "Dillinger was teaching me not to punish others for mistakes people had made in the past. This dog allowed himself to forgive and love again." Dillinger's example inspired Donna to let go of her bitterness and anger.

Angel animals so often have the capacity to help us see life in new and refreshing ways. They're experts at "out-of-the-box" thinking. In the next chapter, you're going to be inspired by the mystical moments angel animals can bring into people's lives.

Chapter Eight

Recognizing Life's Mystical Moments

A *rabbit nestles down*
with its eyes closed
in the arms of a lion.

—Jelaluddin Rumi,
from "Birdsong from Inside
the Egg"

We've received hundreds of stories from people in many walks of life from all over the world. Most depict a moment when the writer and an angel animal have connected spiritually in a memorable way. These mystical moments remind the person that love is all around and life is much more than we can see, feel, and touch.

We've had many mystical moments with animals in our lives. They've helped us connect with our own spiritual nature. The Blessing of the Animals, conducted by many churches on or near October 4, the feast of Saint Francis, patron of animals, honors the sacredness of all God's creatures.

Taylor's Blessing

Taylor sat in the pew between us. Her face held a look of curiosity and amazement. Our yellow Labrador retriever had never been in a church before and Saint Mark's Episcopal Cathedral in Minneapolis was a magnificent one to host her first visit. Beautifully detailed stained glass windows reached up to the high ceilings conveying solid tradition. Taylor seemed to sense that something special was about to happen. She sat spellbound or maybe just overwhelmed. After all, this was not the usual destination for her morning walk.

Hundreds of dogs, cats, birds, hamsters, iguanas, and ferrets waited inside boxes, sat next to their cherished people, or were draped over human shoulders as the sermons, songs, and barking resonated throughout the massive cathedral. To close the church service, a zebra, a falcon, and a camel led a procession down the middle aisle to the front where a minister intoned the liturgy for the Blessing of the Animals.

After singing and liturgy in the cathedral, all the animals and people walked across the street to Loring Park where we followed white-robed priests and joined two other churches that had had similar services. We walked with Taylor close behind the priests with hundreds of animals and humans behind us. Smiles on the priests' faces conveyed their obvious joy and the love they felt at giving service to the animals in this way. When we arrived in the park, a musical group from Ecuador played wind instruments accompanied by an occasional howling dog.

The ministers and priests each dispersed to tents with people and animals lining up to receive their blessings. As the priest blessed the dog in front, Taylor scooped out of her collar and ran to where Allen stood, preparing to take her picture. He explained to her that the blessing is a special event to honor her and that she might enjoy it. She settled down and returned to where Linda stood in line. When it was her turn, Taylor stepped up to the priest, who looked amused. He leaned over and gently touched Taylor's forehead while offering a blessing that brought tears to Linda's eyes. He said, "May the God who made you bless you and keep you." Taylor solemnly accepted the gift with her eyes wide open and her tongue hanging out.

As Linda and Taylor left the line, a woman with a thick European accent said, "She will always be with you now." And so she will. Our love for each other is the forever kind.

In this chapter, angel animals remind us of the invisible side of life, the spiritual element that we often ignore in the frenzied pace of daily living.

Jan sells nutritional supplements for human and animal health and longevity. She enjoys herbal gardening, singing, camping, hiking, visiting zoos, and meeting wildlife in nature. Her volunteer work includes feeding and caring for stray animals and helping at her church. She shares her home in Seattle, Washington, with Pumpkin and Tootsie, two feral cats she tamed as kittens, and Yoda, a stray cat she says is a very flexible and old soul. Jan's amazing story takes us to new realms of angel animal mystical moments with insects.

Guardian Angel Bees

JAN WARREN

It seemed like a situation of the bees versus human invaders. At least, that's what I concluded on a journey into bee territory outside a small town in Oregon. I'd been attending a health convention in a nearby city when I heard about a ranch where underground springs were said to produce 100 percent pure water that contained no minerals or animal residues. I decided that I wanted to bring home a few gallon jugs of this pure water.

When I arrived at the ranch, I could see that getting to this water was going to be quite a challenge. I'd have to climb slippery rock formations to find spots where I could fill my gallon jugs. As I began the journey, I could hear people yelling, "Ouch!"

They were being stung by bees, who were keeping intruders from gathering water at the best places.

I Made Friends with the Bees

After listening to all the moaning as people were getting stung, I decided that my best course of action would be to make friends with these bees and give them the proper respect that they required and deserved. After all, the bees were guarding their home.

So I began to carefully climb to a rock, then I'd wait and inwardly, through thought and from my heart, ask the bees if I could have their permission to go to the next spot. Within a few minutes, the bees would leave the place where I wanted to go and allow me to proceed. All around me, people were forcing their way onto the rocks and getting bitten. But rock by rock, I climbed to a breathtakingly beautiful area where springs gushed up from a sandy bottom and gleamed in the sunlight.

At this spot, I began to lose my nerve, because hundreds of bees swarmed at the center of the pure water source. I couldn't imagine how I'd get to it without being stung.

Again, I waited, inwardly told the bees my intentions, and asked permission to step into their space. To my amazement, the busy, loud, buzzing insects moved away. Gratefully, I stepped up to this prime spot and collected pure water into my containers. My heart overflowed with gratitude for this gift from the bees.

After I finished collecting the golden liquid, I went down the hill the same way I'd climbed it. Each step along the way, I'd silently communicate with the bees and ask them to allow me to take the next step. Surprisingly, they didn't bother me at all, but let me move from rock to rock.

Why Did the Bees Guard the Water So Fiercely?

After my experience, I learned that this thousand-year-old area had been sacred to Native Americans. This is why, as I entered and moved about in it, I could feel the land virtually singing with sacredness. How many generations of bees had protected this territory that Native Americans had loved and revered in the best way they knew how? Did the Great Spirit give bees the task of preventing the profane from trampling on it?

By using the Native American way of approaching nature, with respect and gratitude, I'd been able to demonstrate to the bees that I was in tune with the holiness of the place. I hadn't assumed that it was my inherent right to take this land's waters without asking their blessing.

My experience with the bees taught me that if I approach any plant, insect, animal, or human with love and respect, I'll be recognized as someone who honors the rights and worth of every soul. And I'll be respected and honored in return.

A Drop to Drink: Are mystical moments with the bees or other angel animals teaching all of us how to journey through life with more reverence and respect? Must those who approach our space treat us with the dignity we deserve?

This is Linda's personal story of a mystical moment with an angel ani-mal who used creative imagination.

The Elephant Learned to Fly

LINDA ANDERSON

One sunny afternoon, a friend of mine and I visited a large zoo that is well known for providing education about animals to the public, preserving endangered species, and placing animals in their natural habitats. Although this is a fine zoo that seemed to have made every attempt to achieve its goals of keeping animals in its care comfortable, as we walked around, I found myself feel-ing sad. I sensed that I was picking up on some of the animals' pain. Many of the animals at this zoo have had to endure changes that would devastate anyone—losses that have left them bereft and lonely. Some have been removed from their homes. Others suffer even in these spacious areas from being in captivity. Many long for a freedom that they instinctively crave.

We stood outside an area where a group of elephants milled around aimlessly. As my friend and I marveled at the majesty of these magnificent creatures, one elephant came to the forefront. She stood directly in front of us and looked as if she wanted to communicate. Her large, expressive eyes seemed to bore into me. I suddenly became aware that she was "talking" to me by flashing images. In my mind's eye, I could see how she longed for the wide-open spaces of the homeland where she could roam freely.

Could I Help This Elephant Cope with Change?

This elephant could hardly bear the loss of her freedom. I wondered if I could help my new animal friend use the gift of imagination. I knew a technique that has uplifted me so I can see the spiritual aspects of a situation, especially when I've had to go through changes that were thrust upon me.

I formed images for the elephant and sent them to her telepathically, showing her how to imagine her native land. I explained that she could daydream and visit her beloved home using everything but her physical body. She could be there instantly in thought, feeling, memory, and spirit.

As I continued to communicate, the elephant closed her eyes and swayed her trunk. Then she lifted her front legs, first left, then right, and danced with joyful abandon. She moved so gracefully and with such happiness that her performance began to draw the attention of others. I knew from the blissful look on her face that she'd made her first flight back home, minus the airplane. Her dance reflected her spiritual journey. She'd discovered that nothing could imprison the spirit.

When my friend and I walked away, our elephant sister followed us as far as she could along the barrier that kept her on one side of the fence and us on the other. But we had leaped over this fence, as spiritual beings. Her noble spirit had gone on a flight to freedom, which she could make as often as she wished.

I waved good-bye. She swung her trunk at me in return. I thanked this angel animal for reminding me that we can all use the spiritual tool of creative imagination for coping with even life's most devastating changes.

An Idea to Try: Would you like to have a moment as mystical as the elephant's? If so, envision yourself somewhere that you really want to be. Put all your love into this daydream. Now, fly with the elephant and return to your homeland, wherever that may be.

Jackie is a grandmother from Lodi, California. She calls her avocation of rescuing Labrador retrievers something she'd have to pay someone to let her do if it weren't a volunteer job. Jackie's story introduces us to a mystical moment with an angel animal and a woman who needed to know that miracles are possible.

Molly's Miraculous Return

JACKIE GILSON

Since I have experience with Labrador retrievers, I started the Central California Labrador Retriever Rescue. The only nearby Labrador rescue service concentrated on the Bay Area, and the need in the central valley was great enough to warrant our having our own organization. My first rescue assignment provided me with the inspiration to keep trying to find and place dogs that are abandoned and desperately in need of homes.

The Sacramento County Animal Shelter called to tell me that a nice black male and an older yellow female Lab needed homes. I went to the shelter to take pictures of the dogs so I could feature them on my web site.

The night after I took photos at the animal shelter, I got a call from a woman whose blind sister, Deborah, had lost her Labrador. She asked if I knew of a quiet, older Lab who could be a companion for her sister. Since I'd just met the nice older yellow female at the Sacramento shelter, I thought of this dog immediately.

"What's the dog's name?" the woman asked.

"Molly," I answered.

There was silence on the other end of the line and then a very deep breath. After a moment, the woman told me her sister's story.

A Stolen Dog and a Broken Heart

A caregiver who had been referred to Deborah by her social worker had allegedly presented false credentials to gain entrance to the homes of blind people with the intent of robbing them. This person had taken Deborah's dog, Molly, thinking that she could sell her. When she found that she couldn't make any money, she brought Deborah's dog to the Sacramento shelter and left Molly there.

As often happens with abandoned dogs, Molly, who was eight years old, was scheduled to be euthanized. Deborah's social worker called the shelter and was told, incorrectly, that Molly had been put down. But for some reason, one of the shelter's officers had canceled the order to have Molly euthanized. Instead, she asked a volunteer to call my new Labrador rescue service and try to find a home for the dog. I went right away to get Molly and take her to Deborah.

I'll never forget the feeling of pure joy flowing from Molly when she stood up in the back of my car as we turned down Deborah's street. She wagged her tail so hard that I could barely get a lead on her. When I stopped in front of Deborah's house, Molly jumped out of the car and dragged me to the blind woman's door. Needless to say, there were plenty of tears all around as Molly and Deborah reunited.

Whenever I see abused and neglected Labs that I can't save, I think of Molly as my "warm blankie," which is what my daughter used to call the shred of old blanket she used for cuddling. Each time my grandchildren greet me with, "Have you saved any dogs this week, Grandma?" I think of the miraculous moment when two best friends found each other against all odds. What could be better than that?

> **A Tail to Wag:** Has an angel animal helped you experience mystical moments of gratitude when you recognize the divine order in life?

Karen is a freelance writer from East Jordan, Michigan, who worked for many years as a news writer and photographer. She lives with two cats and one dog who thinks he's a cat. In her story, an angel animal rescues his friend in a mystical moment.

How a Stubborn Horse Saved Sam's Life

KAREN DONALDSON

From the time she was seven years old, my eldest daughter wanted a horse. She even offered, if her dream came true, to keep the horse in her bedroom. Since we still lived in the city, I told her that she could have a horse when she'd worked and saved enough money to buy one and pay a year's room and board for him—in advance.

With this incentive, my daughter, then eleven years old, started working. She did odd jobs, peddled newspapers, and even scrubbed tombstones in a cemetery. When my daughter was thirteen, she fulfilled her wish. A few days after Bo's Moonlight Dusk (Dusky) was born, she bought the golden-toned quarter horse stallion colt, whose sandy color changed to almost black by the time he was a three-year-old. My daughter hand-raised and trained the horse.

Of course, my husband and I didn't allow Dusky to live in our daughter's room, as she'd fantasized. We boarded him with Sam, a friend, and his family until we moved to our own place in the country. As we all got to know Dusky, we began to see how well the horse related to humans.

For example, Dusky was great with kids. Once, one of Sam's children was reported missing. The searchers found the little one playing between Dusky's feet in his stall. The horse was rigid from holding still for such a long time and was greatly relieved when he could safely move his feet after the child was retrieved.

Dusky Worked with Sam

Dusky had his personality quirks. When my daughter wasn't there, Sam took care of the horse. He and Dusky had an understanding. Sam would share his morning coffee with Dusky, who would drink it right from the cup with cream and sugar, of course. They also shared bottles of soda pop and snacks. But when Sam would try to ride Dusky, the horse would do his best to buck him off, despite their real affection for each other. After this showdown, Dusky would nudge Sam as if to say, "Let's do it again."

One day Dusky demonstrated his true affection for Sam and proved to us that animals and humans can work as partners. Sam was setting a tall utility pole in the pasture. Apparently, he didn't make the anchor hole deep enough. Dusky stood nearby and watched as Sam wrestled the pole into the hole and turned to pick up his shovel.

Suddenly, the pole started to fall on Sam!

Sam's wife was doing the dishes and watching from her kitchen window, but she was too far away to rush out and save her husband or to even shout a warning. She froze in terror, knowing that Sam would be badly injured.

Just as the pole started to fall, Dusky grabbed Sam by the seat of his pants and yanked his friend backward! The pole crashed down exactly where Sam had been standing.

Dusky got an extra cup of coffee that day.
But he still wouldn't let Sam ride him.

A Tail to Swish: Has an angel animal shown you how to be
there for a friend in a moment when you're needed the most?

*Bianca is a wife, mother, and grandmother who loves animals, nature,
and music. She used to speak before many audiences about her experiences as a concentration camp survivor. The story Bianca shares
below shows an angel animal who went beyond training to show
compassion. We haven't included an afterthought following this story
because it is one you'll want to reflect upon in your own way. This
story moved us deeply and is one we will never forget.*

The Quality of Mercy

Bianca Rothschild

Animals have always been part of my life. I love them with a
passion. But one special "angel animal" will remain in my heart
forever.

I am a lady in my mid-seventies who has an amazing story to
tell. Born in Poland, I was a teenager when World War II began.
My family always had pets. All of us loved them dearly. When
the Nazis forced us to leave our home to be put into prison, we
entrusted the animals to friends for safekeeping.

By 1945 I was separated from my family and imprisoned in

the Ravensbruck, a concentration camp in Germany. Starving, dressed only in a flimsy uniform, I had to work in the bitter cold. Every day prisoners at the camp congregated in the early morning and waited outside to be counted. One day, while I waited in line, exhaustion and cold overwhelmed me and I fainted. Although two of my friends stood in the long row on either side of me, they couldn't help.

When the Nazi soldiers saw me lying on the ground, they took one of their large German shepherd dogs off of his leash, removed the dog's muzzle, and commanded him to attack. As the dog ran toward me, the prisoners looked on in horror, fully expecting the animal to rip me apart.

But something miraculous happened in that moment.

When the huge dog reached me, he stopped in his tracks. Then he smelled me. To everyone's amazement, the dog, instead of attacking me, licked my face until I revived.

Everyone in the line stood frozen with fear. The soldier who had sent the dog to kill me looked incredibly puzzled. After a minute, I staggered to my feet. Shocked that the dog had allowed me to live, the soldier called the vicious-looking animal back to him.

Those many years ago, an animal befriended me in an insane world of human hatred. I am alive today because a dog disobeyed the command to destroy and instead showed compassion. Was it fate? Was he an angel? I will never know. But to this day I have never forgotten the dog's act of mercy. For the rest of my life I have done whatever I could to save all living creatures.

Doreen holds a doctoral degree in counseling psychology. A very important part of her family is Romeo, a Himalayan cat with a strong personality. Doreen also loves to feed the wild mourning doves, sparrows, and other birds in her Southern California backyard. As part of Doreen's work as a spiritual counselor, she frequently recommends that her clients spend regular amounts of time outdoors, communing with nature. The author of more than a half-million books in print worldwide, Doreen recounts her mystical experience with an angel animal in her book The Lightworker's Way: Awakening Your Spiritual Power to Heal and Know.

The Sea Lion Who Taught Me the Power of Praying Together

DOREEN VIRTUE, PH.D.

I was raised in the Christian Science church, a New Thought religion blending Christianity and Eastern mysticism. Growing up, I'd heard my share of taunts about my family's religion. Some people even insinuated that my faith was un-Christian. I tried not to take such criticism personally, since I felt secure about my beliefs within my heart. Besides, after becoming an adult, I attended different churches, both traditional and nontraditional. Each place offered me something of value, but alone none of the them echoed my deepest beliefs. I did my best to see the divine spark of God within each person I encountered, regardless of whether that person shared my spiritual beliefs. Although people of various faiths pray differently from each other, I'd always felt that when we pray, we're all drinking the same water from which miracles spring.

A Sea Lion Helped Me Understand
Religious Differences

A tiny baby sea lion helped me to really know that we are all one in spirit, and that praying together unites our hearts in a powerful way. As I was walking on the beach near my Newport Beach, California, home, I saw a small brown animal as I neared a long row of rocks known as "The Wedge." Soon I recognized it as a baby sea lion, and I saw that something was wrong with him.

I sat on the sand next to the sea lion. With his flippers, he pulled himself closer to my side. The little guy's breathing seemed terribly labored, and I sensed his exhaustion and fear. I remembered that a large group of sea lions lived on a floating platform off the end of The Wedge and were hovering nearby, looking toward shore where the baby was stranded. I assumed that the baby must have been separated from his mother. Intuitively, I placed my hands above the sea lion and visualized Christ energy coming in through my head, out of my fingertips, and into his tiny body. I prayed for assistance from Jesus and the angels.

Just then, a lifeguard rushed to my side. With a loud voice and abrupt movements, he told me that he'd telephoned an animal shelter to take the sea lion to a marine-life preserve in another seaside town. As he spoke, the sea lion rushed under the shelter of a nearby rock formation. The lifeguard's intense and fearful energy obviously frightened the little animal. The lifeguard took out a stethoscope and attempted to place it on the sea lion's chest. However, the animal hissed and barked as if about to bite. Embarrassed, the lifeguard walked away and mumbled that he'd go watch for the animal shelter truck to arrive.

I realized that something needed to be done. If the animal shelter took the sea lion away, he had little chance of ever reuniting with his mother. I fervently prayed to Jesus for help. As I prayed, the sea lion rejoined me and I continued to send him healing light through my fingertips.

A Young Man Came to Pray for Help with Me

I opened my eyes as a young man gently approached the sea lion and me. The man smiled at me as he carefully sat next to us. The sea lion peacefully remained lying on his side. I explained the situation to the young man and he immediately understood that we needed a miracle if the sea lion was to be reunited with his mother before the rescue truck arrived. A man of faith, he agreed to join me in prayer.

The young man noticed the position of my hands as I prayed. I was still sending healing energy through my fingertips to the sea lion, and he asked, "Are you doing some sort of spiritual treatment?" When I replied, "Yes," he explained that his mother was involved in nontraditional healing and so he recognized that I was conducting "pranic healing" on the sea lion.

When we went back to praying, the young man suddenly said, "Are you sure you're praying to the real Jesus?" He looked at me with a combination of fearful judgment and compassionate concern.

I fingered the crystal cross around my neck and smiled at him reassuringly. "Oh, I'm very sure that I'm talking to the real Jesus."

The young man smiled genuinely back at me, and said, "I guess it's true that whenever two or more are gathered in his name, miracles can happen." I agreed, and we went back to our joint prayers.

Time was running out, though. The animal rescue truck was surely on its way to retrieve the little sea lion.

The Sea Lion Got His Divine Intervention

Then a sound to our left suddenly made us look up. There, on the top of The Wedge, stood a man with long, wild, gray hair. A blinding white light glowed around him, which made it difficult to see his facial features. He climbed down The Wedge rocks surefootedly. Since only an empty parking lot was on the other side of the rocks, it startled me to see him appear out of nowhere.

The man didn't say a word or look at us. We silently watched as he knowingly took charge of the situation. He grabbed a long piece of seaweed and tickled the sea lion's belly. The sea lion protested, but he also moved toward the shoreline a few inches.

My young companion put up his hand, as if to question the older man's actions, but I stopped him and said, "This is good. This is the miracle we prayed for."

The old man continued to tickle the baby sea lion, who responded by inching toward the ocean water. Within minutes, the man had coaxed the little animal back into the sea. His task finished, the man walked away without looking at us or speaking.

The young man and I sighed as we watched the sea lion swim in the direction of the floating platform. Soon the little fellow was reunited with his family. We smiled as he swam away with them. Five minutes later, the animal shelter truck pulled onto the beach sand. My companion and I agreed that we'd witnessed a miracle. I then hurried to catch up with the old man and thank him for his kindness, but he shrugged off my attempts to compliment his actions. Instead, he waved me along with a smile that conveyed, "Go in peace." I walked away from him thinking, *This man is an angel.* And silently I gave thanks for such a remarkable response to the loving prayers that the young man and I had offered together.

My life *was* becoming more peaceful, as I was learning to focus on the similarities that unite me with all people, regardless of their faith. It took a tiny animal to really show me the way!

I had learned from a sea lion that God hears all prayers and answers them in the most unexpected ways when we pray together from our hearts.

A Wave to Ride: In this mystical moment, could the miracle have been as much about offering the opportunity for more understanding between Doreen and the young man as about saving the sea lion? Do angel animals carry out divine assignments designed to heal?

Maryse is an eleven-year-old girl from Sainte Foy, Quebec, Canada. She says that she loves all animals, likes to speed skate, enjoys traveling, and is learning Chinese. Her special animal companions are hamsters. Maryse's story introduces an enterprising hamster who devised a mystical way to express gratitude.

Pucette Found a Way to Say, "Merci!"

Maryse Gauthier

As long as I can remember I've always dreamed of having an animal in my house. I wanted a creature to play with and talk to, especially after school or when I felt alone or sad.

My father didn't want to buy a hamster. He couldn't imagine why I wanted to have such an animal. Mostly, he wanted to be sure that I would take care of a pet, feed it properly, and clean its cage.

To my surprise, for my ninth birthday, my father finally allowed me to have a hamster. I was so happy. We checked in the newspaper to see if there were any for sale, but couldn't find one. So, we went to a pet shop with a lot of hamsters to choose one for me. At that time, I didn't have information about this kind of pet, so it was difficult for me to decide. My father was losing patience. He pointed to one with his finger and said, "Take this one and you'll have fun." I decided to do what he said before he changed his mind.

I named my hamster Pucette, which in French means "little flea." Pucette was a cinnamon Syrian shorthair with large, dark eyes. Pucette liked when I carried her around in my pocket.

I Thought I'd Lose Pucette

My brother started sneezing a lot after we brought Pucette home. My mother took him to the doctor, who prescribed some tests. One week later, what I feared most happened: The doctor said that my brother was allergic to animals.

The doctor asked if we had animals at home. He said my brother's allergy wasn't too serious, so my parents decided to let me keep Pucette. Since I had come so close to losing her, I was very grateful for this decision. Later, I was to see that Pucette was also grateful.

Pucette's cage was in the living room on a table a few feet from a bay window. The kitchen was next to the living room, and a staircase led downstairs to a playroom. At the end of this lower floor, we had a bedroom for visitors. In the other part of the basement, there was a furnace, freezer, gardening tools, a lawn mower, and sporting equipment.

One evening, I decided to sleep in the basement bedroom. Like any hamster, Pucette often tried to escape, but she only went to the basement if I carried her in my hands. On this night, though, a few days after our visit to the doctor's office, Pucette got out of her cage.

In the middle of the night, I smelled an odor of oil and felt something on my neck. I thought it was a rat and I screamed loudly enough to wake my parents, who were sleeping on the main floor. My father ran to check on me. He turned on the light, looked at my neck, and told me, "Don't panic, it's your hamster."

This surprised me because Pucette had to go down twelve steps, find me in the basement bedroom, and climb onto my neck. I noticed that Pucette's body was oily. I figured out that she must have walked across the lawn mower and gotten oil on herself. After cleaning her, I returned Pucette to her cage. It was a special moment. I think Pucette was trying to say "thank you." She wanted to tell me with her visit that she was happy to be in our home and that she was glad we decided to keep her, even if my brother was allergic.

There was one more interesting thing about Pucette's adventure that night. The following spring, we didn't have any problem starting our lawn mower. Every other spring we always had to have it tuned up for it to run again. I believe that Pucette, with her magic touch, repaired our lawn mower!

A Whisker to Twitch: Is an angel animal showing the power of gratitude by taking you beyond your cage/cubicle/box?

More Mystical Moments

Through their spiritual qualities, angel animals offer us the opportunity to have moments of spiritual connection with them, each other, and creation.

In "Eugene Finds a Home," Joyce Stoffers, an assistant professor of English who lives in Weatherford, Oklahoma, writes that a stray mutt followed her home one day and scrambled over the yard fence. Although she unhitched the gate, hoping he'd leave, when she awakened on Easter morning, the dog was sitting at her back door, wagging his mangy tail and looking at Joyce with doleful eyes. Beside him were some gifts for her—a newspaper, a shoe, and a bag filled with daffodil bulbs that he must have picked up from a neighbor's yard.

In that instant, when Joyce delighted in the dog's persistence and ingenuity, she decided to help the little fellow get healed before finding a home for him. She moved him into the doghouse that had been left behind by former owners of her home. After weeks of treating the dog for mange, deworming him, and giving him good food, she named him Eugene, after Saint Eugene Church where he had first started following her.

She concludes her story by saying, "I found a good home for him. Mine."

In part three, you're going to meet some amazing angel animals who teach us about living, dying, and returning to life.

Part Three

WHAT ANGEL ANIMALS TEACH US ABOUT DEATH, DYING, AND THE AFTERLIFE

Being close to animals and experiencing the world as they do has taught me about harmony. They do not shut out their surroundings. They do not close themselves off to sights, smells, and sounds. And as naturally as they open themselves to the surrounding sounds, they open themselves to the surrounding feelings.

—Margot Lasher

Reading about death, dying, and the afterlife might sound depressing, but when you read the next chapters, you're going to find that the opposite is true. Although the stories are moving and many of them brought us to tears, the overwhelming result of reading them is to feel inspired.

In these chapters, you're going to learn that

- angel animals find ways to say good-bye and they let humans know that it's time for them to leave
- angel animals assure us that they'll greet us in heaven
- angel animals return to those they love

You're about to discover proof that love survives.

Chapter Nine

Saying Good-bye in Our Own Way

There was never a King like Solomon,
Not since the world began.
But Solomon talked to a butterfly
As a man would talk to a man.

—Rudyard Kipling, from
"The Butterfly That Stamped"

*A*ngel animals say good-bye in spiritual ways that we might miss if we allow our minds to overrule what our hearts feel. We call the following story "Saying Good-bye to Feisty." It holds a special place in our memories.

For days before the death of our cat Feisty, he visited us spiritually in dreams and during times of prayer and quiet reflection. He told us that he no longer wanted to stay here. He waited until Linda was out of town, so she wouldn't have to be the one to find him. After Allen left for work one day, Feisty went to his favorite spot, lay down quietly in the corner, and left. Only his lifeless shell remained when Allen arrived home.

On the morning of Feisty's death, Linda felt his spiritual presence. She asked him, "Feisty, don't you want to stay here and help us with our new project?" He replied, "I'll be helping from the other side." And this is how *Angel Animals* got its very own guardian angel to help us meet the most wonderful people on the planet and the most inspiring angel animals in the world.

How an Angel Animal Deer Said Good-bye

In Maxine Wilson's story "Deer at the Window," we see how angel animals in nature can appear when we most need them. Maxine, a homemaker from Boulder, Colorado, writes that near the mountains where they lived, she and her husband often took sleeping bags to their patio and slept there. They always awakened to the comforting sight of deer standing next to them, as if they'd been watching over the couple all night. When Maxine's husband died, she writes, "We came home after the memorial service. I looked out the kitchen window. A deer came up to the edge of the patio. He looked in the window and right into my eyes. I could hear the words, 'Everything will be all right.'"

The following remarkable stories express the many ways angel animals say good-bye to the humans that they love. If you've gone through the experience of losing a beloved pet, we hope you'll find them as inspiring and hopeful as we do.

Bob lives in Chico, California, where he plans to practice as an animal defense lawyer. Before he became an attorney, he was a TV news reporter, anchor, and producer. His animal companions Imelda and Sid, two guinea pigs, share a cage in his home. Bob's angel animal helped him graciously say good-bye to his father.

A Guinea Pig Gave Me Precious Time with My Dying Father

Bob Marshall

Imelda entered my life in late spring, soon after I moved my father to California following my mom's death. The runt of a guinea pig litter, Imelda was missing about half of each ear. Despite her chewed-up ears, she was quite the cuddler, and quickly started purring when I picked her up. The guinea pig's feet were all different colors. My wife suggested naming her Imelda because, like her namesake Imelda Marcos, it looked as if she couldn't decide which pair of shoes to wear.

Dad was a very tall and thin man. His amazing, long, graceful fingers were one of his most remarkable features. Dad loved Imelda, so I used to take her to visit him. He'd cradle her carefully in his hands when he petted her. He always had some fresh fruit or vegetables as a treat for the guinea pig.

Dad Didn't Answer the Phone

One Saturday, I called Dad to say I was on my way to take him shopping. He often forgot about it when we had plans to meet, but still, I was concerned this day when he didn't answer the telephone. I drove to his apartment and found him lying on the dining room floor. His face was frozen in a fixed gaze and his left hand moved in a strange, circular pattern.

After the ambulance ride to the hospital, the emergency room exam revealed that the mass in Dad's lung, which doctors feared might be lung cancer, had spread to his brain. The doctors said that Dad had "days to weeks, most likely days, to live."

I stayed with Dad at the hospital as long as I could, but I had to go home to sleep. Besides, I found it emotionally draining to sit and watch that repetitive motion of his left hand.

On Sunday afternoon, my wife tucked Imelda in her purse and smuggled the guinea pig into the hospital. We held her out and said, "Dad, Imelda is here to visit." Until this time, although his eyes had opened, we hadn't seen anything that looked like a real connection. But with Imelda's arrival, Dad opened his eyes, looked directly at the guinea pig, and reached for her. Because his attempts to pet were more of a jerky grasp, we couldn't let him hold her, but I placed Imelda in position so she could cuddle up against his skin, where she purred happily.

On Sunday evening, Dad started talking, but even if his sentences started well, they trailed off into nonsense. Through Monday night, he seemed happy. Some depression and frustration started on Wednesday. I think he didn't want all of the fuss and attention he was getting. On Friday morning, before we were to bring him home, Dad started having seizures. The nurse used medication to bring them under control. On November 22, at about 12:30 P.M., Dad passed away while I held him in my arms.

I firmly believe that wonderful little piggie gave Dad the strength to find his way out of the dark and back into the light to spend a few more precious days with us!

> **A Tail to Swish:** Is there an angel animal who could help you say good-bye to someone you love? Do you have an angel animal companion who could visit a hospital or nursing home and bring the patients there more joy and a sense of connection?

Eleanor recently retired from Burlington–Northern–Santa Fe Railroad, where she worked for thirty years. She loves to read, walk on windy days, watch old movies, and write poetry at her home in St. Paul, Minnesota. Since 1994 Eleanor has had two wonderful male cats who are great pals. Hanki is a black and white tuxedo and Ebeni is a soft, all-black longhair. Eleanor's story reminds us that angel animals can show us how to leave in the most loving ways.

A Cat Let Me Know How Much I Meant to Him

ELEANOR JANE BRIEST

One day, more than twenty-three years ago, I was riding home through the countryside, returning to St. Paul after a visit to my mother's farm. I was gazing out the passenger window at the scenery when I noticed movement in an empty field. I shouted and asked the person who was driving to stop. I don't know why I had such an urge to do so, but I jumped out of the car, ran to a ditch, and started chasing the creature I'd seen from the window. I even rolled under a barbed wire fence to follow what, at closer range, looked like a good-sized cat.

Each time I'd approach the cat, he'd veer away. Then, suddenly, he stopped, turned, and ran up to me as if he'd been waiting for my arrival. I zipped open my jacket, put him inside, and took the cat to the car.

When we got home later that night, I realized that I didn't have enough food in the house to feed the cat, so I gave him some leftovers to tide him over until I could get more food. The next day I took him to the vet, who asked if the cat was eating. I assured him that he was. Then he looked at the cat's feet and said, "He's going to get much bigger. When a cat is dumped out on the road, sometimes a bobcat or lynx mates with her. It looks as if this cat came from such a mating." So, that's how Bobbi got his name, short for bobcat.

Bobbi Always Took Good Care of Me

Bobbi turned out to be an extraordinarily intelligent creature. Because of his ancestry, he could show a vicious streak with others but was always loving and trusting with me. He grew to be the size of a small German shepherd and weighed forty-five pounds. Bobbi carried himself with his head held high, flashing his gorgeous eyes. When I walked him around the neighborhood, I never had to be afraid. Bobbi looked powerful and was not a creature to be messed with. Even in the house, if someone raised his voice or sounded angry, Bobbi would puff and hiss. I always felt protected by him.

I'd often take Bobbi back out to the country when I visited my mother. She grew to love him and considered herself to be his grandma. On these visits, Bobbi would disappear into the bushes and roam the thick trees. He was a strange mixture of feral and domesticated cat. As much as he loved the outdoors, he didn't claw anything in my mother's house, only scratching things she set outside for him.

"I Loved You So"

Late in 1992, I noticed that Bobbi's health seemed to be deteriorating. He was losing weight, but he rallied for the holiday season. But on January 20, 1993, we had an unforgettable, terrible sleet storm. It was very difficult for me to drive on streets like sheets of glass. When I finally made it home, I knew somehow that this was Bobbi's last day with me, and he'd waited until I could be with him before leaving.

I sat quietly with Bobbi's head on my shoulder. In my mind, I spoke to him and could hear him talking to me. Very distinctly, I heard Bobbi say, "The gate is open."

I looked at this unique cat who had spent twenty-three years loving and protecting me. As hard as it was to do, I said good-bye to him with the words, "Go quickly."

As Bobbi exhaled his final breaths, I heard him whisper to me in my heart, "I loved you so."

I had Bobbi's body cremated and his ashes placed in an urn. My pastor has assured me that she'll have his ashes put in my casket when I'm buried. This seems fitting, for Bobbi was much more than a cat to me. I believe that Bobbi was an ambassador God sent to love and protect me. Ever faithful at his post, Bobbi has been called back home. My mother said that Bobbi took good care of me right until the end, and that he died in my arms at home because he knew it would have been too difficult for me to have had to put him to sleep. As she said, I had a creature who could leave me with the parting words, "I loved you so."

A Paw to Lick: Is there someone, an animal or a human, who needs to hear from you Bobbi's final words, "I loved you so"? Can you let others know, before it's time to say good-bye, how much you value and cherish them?

Damaris has two children and three grandchildren. She enjoys basket-ball, horseback riding, and hiking through a forest near her home in Matherville, Illinois. She works as a buyer in the pharmacy of a local medical center. Her inspiring story offers the possibility that, in very spiritual ways, angel animals prepare us for their departure.

Dreaming My Farewell to Springer

DAMARIS MILLER

I used to love to raise springer spaniels as a hobby. One of my pups went to a friend who named her Springer. Eventually, my friend got a divorce and seemed to have little time to give to the beautiful spaniel. When I would go out in the morning, Springer would be there waiting for me. The pup seemed to adopt us, so we welcomed her back into our family.

Springer became a valuable friend to my two daughters and me. She was always giving us love and support. As the years went by, things changed. I went through a lengthy divorce. Springer always seemed to know when to put her head in my lap and just give love.

In her sixteenth year, Springer started having health prob-lems. One day my daughter called and said Springer was bumping into things. When I came home from work, I thought that the dog must have had a stroke. I took her to the vet, who said we could give Springer some medication but, in addition to the stroke, she had congestive heart failure.

I Couldn't Say Good-bye

I talked with Springer about what was happening. I realized that the time had come for her to move on, but it seemed impossible for me to let her go. I cried a lot and kept asking Spirit to help me. I knew I should have Springer put to sleep, but I just couldn't do it.

Over the next month, Springer was patient with my unwillingness to say good-bye to her. I spent most nights on the kitchen floor holding her and wishing she could stay with me.

One night I had the following dream:

> I see myself taking Springer to the veterinary clinic. My favorite vet, whom I haven't seen for four or five years, is there. As she gives Springer a lethal injection, the dog's head slumps in my arms. Through my tears I say, "Is she gone?"
>
> Dr. Bonnie says, "Yes." All of a sudden, Springer raises her head and looks into my eyes as if to say, "Good-bye, for now."
>
> I then receive a silver ring from Dr. Bonnie. The inscription inside reads "Springer." It is a symbol of the love bond we shall always share.

When I awoke from this dream, I knew that Spirit had prepared me for my beloved dog's death. I was hoping Springer would go in her sleep and the decision would be taken out of my hands. The dream helped me to realize that sometimes, perhaps for the spiritual growth the experience will bring, we have to go through a tough situation without an easier way out of it.

Would My Prophetic Dream Come True?

I called for an appointment to take Springer to the vet the next morning. It was a rainy, dark day. I talked to Springer and told her about the adventure she'd be taking by passing over to the other side. I assured her that I'd be with her till the end.

When I got to the clinic, I was shocked to see Dr. Bonnie there, just as she'd been in my dream. As she injected Springer, I held the dog in my arms. I talked to her about the journey she would take. I thanked her for sharing her love with our family. Her head started to slump. It was such an incredible and yet painful feeling to hold my dear friend as she crossed over from this life to the afterlife. Then, exactly as I'd done in my dream, I asked, "Is she gone?"

Dr. Bonnie said, "Yes."

As in my dream, Springer turned around to give me one last look. In it, she conveyed all her gratitude for my letting her go.

The only thing different from that special dream was that I didn't receive a silver ring. But I'll always feel as if one is on my finger, reminding me of Springer's love.

I believe that as we grow, we learn to do things we thought we could never do. By going through some of life's most difficult experiences, we become spiritually stronger and discover that love is more powerful than pain.

Thank you, Springer, for teaching me about love and for coming to me in a dream to prepare me for losing you.

A Tail to Wag: Is it possible that animals can appear in our dreams to prepare us for their passing? Are there more ways of saying good-bye than we ever imagined possible, when we turn to the spiritual realms for comfort and understanding?

Brad lives in Monroe, Washington, where he shares his home with eleven ferrets, two llamas, one horse, two dogs, five cats, two pheasants, twelve chickens, nine doves, tropical fish, and a pond full of pet trout. He likes to go backpacking with his wife and two llamas. His story of an angel animal in a ferret's body shows us another way these wonderful creatures appreciate it when we say good-bye to them in whatever way we can.

Willy Wouldn't Leave Until I Said Good-bye

BRADLEY HILL

When Willy arrived at our home we had ten other ferrets and a new addition, Otis, who joined us the same day. Willy, who had been abused, took a bit of time adapting to his new home. At first, he cried and shook in his sleep. Understandably, he seemed afraid of everything. Soon, though, with lots of love and attention, Willy joined our family.

Willy became the most playful of all our ferrets. He was probably about five or six years old when we got him, and all his friends were just two, so this made him the older brother. Willy played hard, but when it was time for bed, he'd find his favorite place in the closet, usually on top of our horse's saddle, and fall asleep.

Willy's Health Declined

Willy's health improved dramatically after he came to live with us. His scruffy, dull coat became bright and glossy. But after about a year, his health started to decline. One day when I walked by his cage, I noticed that he was standing on his back legs shaking the bars with his front feet. I now know that with this action Willy was telling me that his time to leave was near. This was his way of saying good-bye. I was in a hurry, though, and walked by him. But I remember that he looked right at me, as if he were trying to tell me something.

I found it difficult to watch Willy growing sicker. Finally, we knew he'd soon have to leave us. But I believe that the little fer-ret stayed alive for me. I desperately didn't want him to die.

My wife realized that Willy needed me to tell him that it was all right to move on. So, one day, while Willy lay in her lap, she held a crystal pendulum and circled it above him. She kept re-peating, "Willy, we'll let you go, now. If it's time for your energy to move on, we understand." I watched as his heaving body soon calmed, and he stopped breathing.

We buried Willy next to the grave of our dog, Rhombus, and planted a tree over them.

I believe that our humanity is enhanced to great heights by the love we feel for and get from our pets. I'm grateful for the time we had with Willy. He'll always hold a place in our hearts.

An Idea to Consider: Is it possible that angel animals wait to die until we can handle their departure better? Is there an angel animal or a person who needs you to say good-bye and re-lease him or her into heavenly arms?

Lisa is a short story writer from Pittsburgh, Pennsylvania. She enjoys needlework, gardening, and writing. She says that her current household is composed of animals—Loki, an elkhound; Shadow, a black cat; Bagel, a beige cat nicknamed Pound Cake; Gus, an Abyssinian cat; Bear, a black Labrador mix; and Chloe, a calico cat. Except for Chloe, all the animals are male; they form a family with Lisa and her husband's two teenage sons. Lisa's story, an open letter from her to her mother, shows the spiritual connections that angel animals make between those who leave and the ones who stay behind.

Split Hearts in the Snow

Lisa Chewning

Two days before you died, you sat drinking coffee with my sister at your dining room table in front of the picture window. A white-tailed deer sailed by. He moved so quickly that, at first, you weren't sure you saw him. For years, you'd told me about seeing deer outside this window. You even tried to take photos of them.

I grew up in that house and played in the woods across the street. I watched pheasants, rabbits, salamanders, hawks, snakes, crayfish, field mice, raccoons, and box turtles, but I never saw the deer. We laughed over the fact that you were the only one who could see them.

Ours was a neighborhood of cars and noisy children, of cats with bells around their necks and barking dogs, of whispering sprinklers in the summer, of scraping shovels in the winter, of saxophone music drifting from a neighbor's open window. But when I was a child, I thought we lived in a wild place. A female ring-necked pheasant marched her brood through "the meadow," as you called our backyard, across the street, and into the woods. A baby milk snake found his way into the dining room. A neighbor's son found a baby screech owl with brown, speckled feathers. The owl's shining, frightened eyes glowed when he turned his head to look all around our bright house.

Day after day, one hot summer, we heard the haunting cry of a bird. Dad said it sounded like a child blowing into an empty bottle. I sat in the cool, green shade of our magnolia tree and wondered what creature made the lonely noise. You awakened me at dawn one morning, so I could see the mourning dove who sat on the window ledge. I heard his low, gentle sound, "Coo-ah. Coo, coo."

The Deer Appeared

But of all the animals in "the meadow," the deer were almost mystical in their showings. At first, they came to call infrequently, but in the last few years, they appeared more often. You marveled at their delicate, graceful movements on thin, fragile legs, at their dark eyes, secretive and alert. Even though they were the cause of your tulips and marigolds disappearing, you welcomed them.

Whenever I visited, I stood in your kitchen, next to your warm stove. I rested my forehead against the cold glass of the back door and looked out at the meadow of your yard across the rooftops. I observed all the colors of the setting sun, the church steeple silhouetted against the sky, the puffs of smoke drifting upward from chimneys. I waited to see the deer. I sat at the dining room table and waited for them. They didn't come to see me. But they came to you.

Two days before you died, when a deer dashed by your window, you quietly accepted the gift. Was the deer a buck or a doe? The animal moved so fast that you couldn't tell. This visit was a sign, a message that only you heard and understood.

It snowed the night you died. In the morning, there was a set of hoofprints outside the dining room window. They looked like split hearts in the snow.

Now, I stand in your kitchen, my forehead resting against the cold, back door glass. I look out at your silent meadow, at the bare branches etched against the dusk sky.

And I wait for the deer.

A Footprint to Follow: Could there be so much love in the universe that angel animals, as messengers, leave footprints in our own snowy backyards? Ones that say good-bye and prove that we don't leave this earth alone? And that we will be missed?

Saying More Good-byes

Mary Grady-Thorne, a hospice volunteer from Pittsfield, Massachusetts, writes about her angel animal in "Roma and the Dancing Black Bear Reassured Me." She says that on the day her cat Roma, his body eroded by cancer, had a lethal injection, she wrapped him in his fleece blanket, put him in a box with his favorite toys, and buried him at home. She writes, "I felt as though my heart had been torn out of my chest."

The next day was cold and rainy to match Mary's darkness and grief. She went to the kitchen and glanced out the window. She writes, "There was a dancing black bear in my backyard! He was hanging on to the suet feeder, trying to reach the chunks of beef fat inside, and with every revolution of the feeder, around he'd go, swinging to and fro." Mary found herself shrieking and laughing at the youngster's antics.

After the bear finished eating, he walked to the corner of Mary's porch, stood up, gently placed his front paws on the window where she stood, and looked into her eyes. Mary says, "There's no doubt in my mind that Roma let me know that he was still with me by finding a way to make me laugh, even when my heart was aching. And it was symbolic that the bear was sent as the messenger because, in the realm of animal spirits, Bear represents rebirth and introspection." Mary concludes her story by saying, "My experience with Roma has helped me become more sensitive to the influence of spiritual guidance."

The next chapter offers some wonderful examples of how angel animals go through grieving and what we can learn from them spiritually about handling the tough times.

Chapter Ten

Going Through Grieving

johnson

When Coco [an orphaned gorilla] first looked out the window of her pen at a forested mountainside like the one on which she grew up, she suddenly began "to sob and shed actual tears." [Dian] Fossey said she never witnessed a gorilla do this before or afterward.

—Jeffery Moussaieff Masson

*I*n *When Elephants Weep: The Emotional Lives of Animals*, Jeffrey Moussaieff Masson tells the story that he found in *Elephant Tramp*, a book written in 1955 by a trainer named George Lewis. Masson writes that when a shy elephant named Sadie was trained too quickly for an act she was to do in the Robbins Brothers Circus, she had a hard time learning it. One day, she was so upset that she ran from the ring and was later punished for not responding to the training. Sadie began to sob with tears pouring from her eyes. The amazed trainers stopped berating the elephant and hugged her instead. Lewis didn't punish Sadie again. She learned to act, becoming what he called a "good" elephant for the circus.

Sadie had demonstrated an important spiritual truth—it's okay to cry.

Grieving is a natural process that humans and animals go through. We've received many stories and letters from people all over the world who miss their beloved animal companions and grieve for them as they would over the loss of a family member.

As you read this chapter, you're probably going to have to cry at times. We did. But we hope that the inspiring nature of these stories will help you cope with the inevitable loss of your beloved companions.

Mary Kate describes herself as just an ordinary fourteen-year-old from Chesterton, Indiana. Her hobbies include basketball, Rollerblading, reading, photography, writing, and surfing the Internet. Her favorite activity is being on stage, where she loves to sing, dance, and act. She adopted five cats, Figaro, Mitzie, Annie, Duffy, and J.R., from a local cat shelter. Her hamsters, Hazel, HoJo, Sydney, and Rascal, and guinea pigs, Inky and Blinky, complete her current family. Still close to her heart are former pets Joey, Buddha, Lucky, and Squeegie. This story about mice helped Mary Kate understand how angel animals grieve.

A Brokenhearted Mouse Taught Me About Grieving

Mary Kate McKenna

I believe that experience is the hardest kind of teacher; first, it gives you the test, then you learn the lessons. That's what my experiences with animals have taught me. I have five cats, two guinea pigs, and four Russian dwarf hamsters. But this is the sad tale of two mice.

I got my first mouse in a very strange way. At a play practice two years ago, I noticed a boy in the corner who had a Pringles can full of mice. Being an animal person, I asked him what he was going to do with them. "Give 'em to my boa," he said.

I was shocked. I begged him for one. He said, "No." But I was persistent. Finally, I offered him twenty dollars. He told me I was crazy and handed me a black female mouse.

"Great! Now, what?" I asked. I had a hamster at home, but I didn't have any idea about how to take care of a mouse!

I cleared out the small compartment of my backpack and placed the mouse in it. I soaked some bread from my half-eaten sandwich in water and gave it and a dry piece to her.

That day went so slowly. I kept thinking, *How is Mom going to take this?* Finally, it was time to go home from school.

My Mom is also an animal person, so she just smirked when I showed her the mouse after I got into the car. I cried when Mom said that I'd be able to keep the mouse. When we came home, I placed the small animal in my hamster's travel cage and named her Lucky.

The next day I bought a ten-gallon tank and a water bottle for the little mouse. I read about mice all day and found out they often die of loneliness. When I told my mom about this, we got a partner for the mouse that weekend and I named her Squeegie.

The Two Mice Became Great Friends

Immediately, the two mice were best buddies. They slept and played together every day for two years. Usually, mice have a life span of only one year, so I knew they were getting very old. One day I found Lucky dead on the floor of her cage. Squeegie was nearby burying her. This touched me. Here were these little creatures, who can be snake food, caring for and loving each other.

A week later, Squeegie passed away. It was so sad to see my last mouse leave that week. But she had been grieving. It was obvious that Squeegie was very sad. She didn't want to climb or chew on her wood block or run on her wheel. I cried when I saw Squeegie lying in her cage. What really touched me was that she didn't die from a disease or a broken bone but from a broken heart.

I hope I gave Lucky and Squeegie a wonderful two years of life. I know it was much more than they would have had in any pet store or at that boy's house. How people can put even the smallest creature through any kind of torture is beyond me. I believe that animals have personality, souls, and hearts. I could never hurt one.

Later, because of those two mice, I adopted many hamsters to give my love to.

An Idea to Consider: Do angel animals grieve when they lose their friends and family? Could you ease the pain of an animal or person with a broken heart by giving love, attention, and companionship?

Christina is from Bunyip, Victoria, Australia. She shares her observations of how quail offer compassion and hospice to one another.

The Quail Offered Hospice

CHRISTINA LOUISE DICKER

This is a tale of compassion and commitment, which happened as I witnessed an astounding exchange between two tiny birds.

My husband and I kept a pair of quail in our cockatiel aviary. The female was a pearly grey color and the male was an earthy brown. The pair had not been together very long and did not seem particularly enamored with each other.

One afternoon I found the female standing quietly in the corner with her feathers puffed out in the typical manner of an unhealthy bird. The male wasn't paying any attention to her but simply going about his business.

The following morning I encountered a different scene. The two quail stood side by side on the aviary floor. The female, overcome by weakness, had closed her eyes and was leaning heavily against her partner. Standing patiently, he supported her full body weight. I checked on the two birds over several hours, and they hadn't moved. I was touched by this show of dedication from the male bird. He could have chosen to walk away and relieve himself of this burden, but he stayed with his companion and held her up all day, denying his own needs for food and water. The night hours must have sapped her final strength, for I found her dead the next day. The male was once again going about his business.

Had his gesture been an act of love? I cannot say, but certainly he'd shown tremendous loyalty, and his was a deliberate act of compassion. Without a doubt, the physical closeness of the two birds must have given the female some measure of comfort through her final hours.

I was consumed by empathy as I watched this sad story unfold. I learned a vital lesson from the example they showed. Now, when my loved ones need my help, I will strive to give unselfishly and to offer my support in a humble way—the way I was shown by a quail.

Wings to Fly: Could a quail show the importance of physically placing ourselves under the wing (shoulder) of a person or an animal who needs comfort in his or her final hours? Could you consider serving in a hospice program in which caring people listen to and support the terminally ill?

Diane lives near Saint Leonards, New South Wales, Australia. A writer/editor for a government department, Diane enjoys writing, trekking through wilderness areas where she observes wildlife, diving, camping, Latin American dancing, and traveling to exotic places, such as Ecuador and the Galápagos Islands. Her story demonstrates how an angel animal helped her learn an important lesson about the stages of grief.

A Rabbit Showed That We Each Grieve in Our Own Way

Diane Robinson

When I stroke Twinkle's soft, white fur, my rabbit half-closes her eyes and lifts her head in appreciation. If she's done something she knows I won't like, such as gnawing on furniture, she'll kick her legs in the air and look at me archly when I approach her, as if to say, "Sorry, but is it really that important?" Twinkle knows what's important because she taught me a valuable lesson.

I used to have another rabbit, Dinkus, who was also white, although she had black ears, nose, paws, and tail. When I adopted the two rabbits, they were so small that they could each balance on the palm of one hand. The rabbits got on well together and pressed against each other, although Twinkle would go through periods of pulling bits of fur out of Dinkus to show her who was boss. Dinkus was submissive and tolerated Twinkle's bullying, which never lasted long. An affectionate, lively rabbit, who loved to be cuddled, Dinkus would sit on my knee for hours relaxing.

When I gave the rabbits the run of our flat, Dinkus would back up to one wall, then sprint the length of the living room, hallway, and bedroom, jumping and twirling like a circus acrobat. With her bright eyes and pricked ears, she was a showstopper. One of my friends called her Houdini because of her ability to contort herself into all sorts of weird and wonderful positions.

Everyone loved Dinkus.

I tried to treat both rabbits equally, so neither would get jealous, but Dinkus was my favorite. I couldn't help it. She was loving and outgoing while Twinkle was reserved and suspicious. Dinkus loved people; Twinkle tolerated them.

The Rabbit I Preferred Became Ill

Unfortunately, Dinkus was diagnosed with cancer. During her illness, Twinkle would lick the horrible lump on her friend's leg and groom her fur and ears. When Dinkus was finally put to sleep, we didn't show her body to Twinkle. We thought that seeing Dinkus like that would upset Twinkle too much.

Crying, we buried Dinkus in the garden. I grieved over the rabbit, remembering how she'd lick my wrist and tug at my watch strap when I stroked her or jump around in circles on the bedroom rug. I missed her so much.

When I explained to Twinkle what had happened, her ears pricked up as I mentioned Dinkus's name. Later she stayed in the corner of the room with her nose twitching, looking unperturbed. Twinkle didn't seem to grieve over Dinkus. I thought she didn't care. She ate, drank, enjoyed being stroked, and was as quiet and reserved as ever. She didn't seem to miss the furry bunny who, for four years, licked her ears and played leapfrog with her.

I couldn't help but start to dislike Twinkle for her callousness. I did my duty, feeding her and changing the litter, but emotionally, I was withdrawn. Out of my grief over losing Dinkus, I said to my husband, Matt, "If one of the rabbits had to die, why couldn't it have been Twinkle?"

He was horrified by my honesty. "How can you say that?" he admonished. "It's wicked."

I knew that he was right, but I couldn't help how I felt.

Twinkle Taught Me a Lesson About Grieving

About a week after Dinkus died, Twinkle was stretched out on a cushion in the living room watching television with Matt and me, when I noticed a lump on her back leg in almost the same place where Dinkus's tumor had been. Twinkle's lump, sore-looking and ugly, was much smaller than Dinkus's tumor. I didn't sleep that night, terrified that Twinkle had cancer. The next day, I took her to the vet, who examined her. She said that she'd give Twinkle a needle biopsy to find out whether the lump was a tumor or an abscess. She took my trembling rabbit, who hates strangers, into the other room while I waited feeling guilty over my angry feelings toward her.

Because Twinkle hadn't grieved the way I thought she should, I'd presumed she didn't care. I scolded myself about how judgmental I'd been. *She's a rabbit, for goodness' sake*, I thought. *What did you expect her to do, weep, wail, and wear black crepe? She's probably taken on Dinkus's illness out of grief. Or maybe you've wished it on her, and she's subconsciously reacted to emotional neglect. When Twinkle needed comforting, you weren't there for her.*

The vet returned with my rabbit huddled miserably in her arms. She had scarcely walked through the door, when I asked if Twinkle was all right. The vet smiled and said, "She has an abscess."

"It's not cancerous, is it?" I asked.

"No," the vet said, putting Twinkle back into her carrier. "But you'll have to give her antibiotics every day."

In the waiting room, Matt looked up anxiously as we came out of the surgery. He was relieved to hear that Twinkle was going to be all right. We made a fuss over the poor, shivering bundle.

"Do you think," I said, as we went out to the car, "that Twinkle got her lump out of sympathy for Dinkus? Do you think she knows what happened to her and this is her way of apologizing to Dinkus for not sharing her pain?"

"Could be," Matt said.

When we got home, I spent a lot of time stroking Twinkle and talking to her. I told her that I'd been selfish and mean. It had been unreasonable of me to withdraw from her. It wasn't Twinkle's fault that Dinkus had died or that she was a more nervous, less affectionate rabbit than the cute animal with the black ears.

I now knew that Twinkle had grieved a great deal but stoically continued looking after herself while developing external symptoms of her internal pain. So, for the next couple of weeks, we gave Twinkle antibiotics twice a day. The vet said that she wouldn't like the taste of them, and she certainly struggled when we fed them to her, but she never scratched or bit us. She trusted that we were doing the right thing. She didn't blame me for my previous attitude toward her.

This is how a rabbit taught me not to condemn those who are undemonstrative, suspicious, or nervous, for they too have their feelings. Twinkle taught me not to judge others by appearances or jump to hasty conclusions. She showed me that although I hadn't treated her well this one time, she could still trust me.

A Tail to Thump: Incongruent grieving means that we don't all grieve the same way or go through stages of grief at the same times. Are there others who are expressing their grief differently than you? Do they still need your support and understanding?

Leah lives in Kennett, Missouri, with her son. She works for the county sheriff, and her hobbies include showing her standard poodle and dog obedience training. An angel animal parrot found a unique way of helping Leah grieve the loss of a very good friend.

Joe the Parrot Remembered Our Friend

LEAH MOBLEY

When my son was seven years old, he and I accompanied a friend of ours (I'll call him Chuck) to purchase his first pet. Chuck was a fifty-something, hard-drinking, chain-smoking bricklayer. He'd never had a pet. Chuck was uncomfortable around dogs, but his brother and sister-in-law owned an African grey parrot he liked. So Chuck decided that he wanted one for himself.

The parrot that Chuck chose was a baby who was still being hand-fed. The breeder told us a lot about greys and said they had a long life span. I jokingly told Chuck that he'd have to let my son inherit the bird. None of us knew then that, in four months, my friend would be diagnosed with throat cancer.

When Chuck became ill, my little boy and I helped him as much as possible. He lived alone and chose hospice care instead of going to a hospital. His bird proved to be a wonderful companion.

Chuck named the parrot Joe Bilittrul. Those two really bonded. Every morning, first thing, Chuck would give Joe a peanut. For someone who had always made snide remarks about the silly ways of pet owners, Chuck was now acting like a parent admiring his new offspring. He'd comment on how he liked the way Joe's feathers looked, and he enjoyed watching as the bird "put on a show" playing with his toys.

Chuck wanted to hear the parrot talk, but Joe never said a word the whole time he lived with him. Before he died, less than a year after he bought the baby parrot, Chuck gave me the African grey. I would have wanted a young grey under any circumstances, but it was especially significant to receive this one from my dying friend.

Joe Remembered Chuck

Joe linked the past with the present for me as I dealt with grieving the loss of my friend. The bird had a special way of remembering Chuck. During the week of the first anniversary of his death, I'd been thinking a lot about Chuck, although I hadn't been talking about him. Maybe Joe picked up on my thoughts or sensed Chuck's spiritual presence as I reminisced about him. After all, Chuck believed strongly that there is an afterlife. For reasons I'll probably never understand, that week, Joe began to speak in what sounded like Chuck's voice. He said a couple of phrases that were characteristic of the way Chuck expressed himself.

Joe mimics me and my son all the time, but his male vocalizations seem to come from nowhere—or, maybe, from the place where my friend is resting peacefully now.

Wings to Fly: Do angel animals help us commemorate the passing of people or animals we've loved? Could they have their own ways of handling grief that would astound us if we noticed them?

Geri is from Beebe, Arkansas, where she runs a pet-sitting business called Kritter Sitters. She volunteers for the Arkansas K9 Search and Rescue. Geri's remarkable story is about an angel animal who was determined to help her overcome grief.

A Wise Dog Restored My Belief in God

Geri Hough

When my Saint Bernard, Misty, was one year old, I sent her for obedience training at the house of some trainers. The instructors went hunting over the weekend, and while they were gone Misty dug out of the pen they kept her in and wandered into the woods.

Because they thought that Misty might return to them on her own, the trainers didn't notify us that Misty was gone until the following Tuesday. They said a hunter had seen her. By then, we had no idea how to find her and were terrified that she'd be killed. My husband took our male dog into the woods to look for Misty, thinking he might meet her coming home.

On the day Misty dug her way out of the trainers' yard, the stepdaughter of my ex-husband came to see me. She told me that my ex-husband was dying of liver disease. This young girl hadn't seen her father in thirteen years, and she planned to visit him that weekend. It was a shock for me to learn that he was so sick, and I began to grieve over the news.

I Didn't Think I'd See Misty Again

Losing Misty reopened my unhealed wounds. Years earlier, when I was still married to my ex-husband, our child had died from sudden infant death syndrome (SIDS). Since the child's death, I'd lost my faith in God. Now I thought that Misty was going to be one more creature I loved who would be taken away from me. In spite of my anger toward God, each day I prayed for Misty's return. But I truly didn't think I'd ever see her again.

Five days after Misty ran away, my sons, who are seven and eight years old, got off the school bus at our house. They were amazed to find a bedraggled-looking Misty. Excitedly, the children called for me. I dropped to my knees when I saw the dog. I couldn't believe she had survived five days, traveling eight miles through the rough terrain of woods, streams, and lakes, where she'd never been before, to make it back home.

As I hugged Misty, I thanked God and realized that this dog had restored my belief in a God who cares about me. She'd dug her way out on the day I'd been so depressed over grieving about my ex-husband and remembering the loss of my child. It was as if she knew that I needed her. She'd traveled such a long way to deliver the message that I wasn't alone or abandoned.

A Tail to Wag: Do angel animals serve as messengers to let us know that we're loved? Has an angel animal given you hope when you were grieving? Is there someone who is in pain that you could comfort as angel animals so often do?

More About Angel Animals' Grief

For centuries angel animals and humans have joined one another in grieving over the loss of loved ones. The following lines are an excerpt from "In the City of the Dead," a poem by the mystic Kahlil Gibran. Though the words were written decades ago, they express the feelings of many today.

> *The wife whose silent tears bespoke her sorrow,*
> *A baby crying because his mother wept,*
> *and a faithful beast who would follow*
> *also in his dumb grief.*
> *And when these reached the place of graves,*
> *They lowered the coffin down into a pit in*
> *the far corner, well removed from the*
> *lofty marble tombs.*
> *Then they turned back in silence and in*
> *desolation,*
> *And the dog's eyes looked oftentimes toward*
> *the last dwelling-place of his*
> *friend and master,*
> *Until they had disappeared from sight*
> *behind the trees.*

The next chapter offers astonishing stories of angel animals who may cause us to question the finality of death. We hope you'll discover rays of hope filtering through the tears.

Chapter Eleven

Messages from Heaven

Heaven is the place of final and complete happiness God has prepared for us—and if animals are necessary to make us happy in heaven, then you can be sure God will have them there.

—Rev. Billy Graham

We've received many stories of angel animals who let people know, after death, that their love has survived. You'll have to decide for yourself, when you read the stories in this chapter, if angel animals deliver messages from heaven.

In Stephen Collier's story, "Tux Bounces a Message to Us," he shares a special message he received from his cat. Stephen, who lives in Shreveport, Louisiana, writes that Tux's favorite trick was to wait until Steve and his wife, Sally, fell asleep, then take a running jump and bounce off their stomachs. Steve writes, "If a cat could laugh, he was laughing." One night, after Tux had died very painfully following a bout with a rare form of cancer, Steve went to sleep on the couch because his snoring had been bothering Sally. Steve says, "At about 3:30 in the morning Sally and I met in the hall with looks of amusement on our faces. We'd been bounced, feeling that familiar pressure on our stomachs, at about the same time. Since we had no other cat around, we figured Tux had come back to let us know that he's still with us." Steve and Sally talked the rest of the night. They concluded that Tux's visit meant that they needed a cat in the house. Now they have four cats, all rescued from the pound. Steve writes, "After adopting our first cat, Tribble, there were no more night belly bounces. I guess Tux was happy with our additions."

Signs from Heaven

Did you know that smell is a way angel animals communicate after death? In "The Memory of Dennis's Scent," Dale Judith Exton, a social worker from Coleshill, England, writes that her dog, Dennis (the Menace), died about seven years ago. Four years ago on August 21, Dale woke up to the pleasant scent of Dennis as he used to smell after taking a bath. Dale got out her album of doggie photos. After looking at Dennis's records, she saw that the twenty-first of August was the dog's birthday. Dale says that since then she's often felt Dennis's presence, especially when she feels sad and needs some cheering up.

Talana McNeely, who calls herself "The Animal Nanny," shares her story, "JD's Message from Heaven." Talana, who lives in Fremont, California, says that she was devastated over the loss of her dog, JD. Talana says that she prayed for a sign that JD was all right. One day while driving down the road, she writes, "I looked up and saw a cloud formation that looked just like JD running with his ears back, laughing, and having a great time." She interpreted seeing JD in the clouds as a message from heaven. It reassured her that nothing could break the bonds of love that she and JD had shared.

Susan J. Allyn, a volunteer with the Camp Fire boys and girls, is from Baldwinsville, New York. In her story, "Skippy Sits on My Lap One More Time," Susan says that when she came home because her father had died, she ran straight to a tree behind an elementary school. She and her childhood friend Skippy, a golden setter, used to often sit under the tree for many hours, as Susan read aloud to the dog. But after Susan left home to join the navy, Skippy became ill. Susan took a month's leave, spent Skippy's remaining days playing with and loving her best friend, hugged him good-bye, and knew that she'd never see him again. When she sat under their favorite tree and began to cry over her father's death, Susan says, "I felt a weight, as if Skippy were lying with his head on my legs just as he'd done all his life. The feeling comforted me through that difficult time."

As you read the following stories, remember the beloved animals who have blessed you with their presence. If you wish, ask God to help you recognize your own messages from heaven.

Aynne lives in Liverpool, New York. She's an ordained minister, has worked in law enforcement for more than twenty years, and owns and operates an astrology business. Aynne's story provides proof that angel animals let us know their love for us has survived.

A Cat Let Me Know That Love Lives

Aynne McAvoy

My cat, Nike, was killed while walking on a nearby road. I had a special relationship with her, but our three other cats didn't like Nike much. My husband preferred the calico and my daughter liked the tortoiseshell. Nike knew that no one but I favored her, so she behaved worse to get more attention. But I loved her unconditionally, no matter how angry she could make me at times.

Nike was silver gray with tips of white on her four paws and tail. She had a white spot on her belly and one leading down from her chin that always made her look as if she were dribbling milk.

It amused me to see Nike often acting like a wild cat, growling at the canned food in her dish as if it were alive.

Shortly after Nike's death, I called a friend who is an animal psychic and asked if she could contact Nike. My friend said that Nike didn't realize that she was dead and had come back into our front yard just to hang out. My friend said that on the other side a special lady came to help Nike adjust. Her heavenly assignment was to take care of recently deceased cats to help them make the transition between this life and the afterlife.

Upon hearing this news about Nike, I sent her my love with all my heart.

Later that night, after talking to my friend, and for a few nights following, I could hear Nike running up the stairs. I also heard her giving me her usual "hi, there" mew. A few times I even caught a glimpse out of the corner of my eye of Nike curled up on her usual spot on my futon. I found cat tracks on a glass table that Nike used to get up on so she could look outside. (She wasn't supposed to do this, but nothing ever stopped her.) I also found Nike's food scattered all around her dish—she was the only cat in our house who did this.

It's comforting for me to know that even though Nike isn't physically with me, she's still around.

A Paw to Lick: Will we meet our animal companions on the other side? Can the bonds of love that were so special in life transcend death? If a beloved animal has passed away, would you like to close your eyes and send love to your friend? Let yourself feel the love moving in waves between you and the angel animal you miss so much. Take comfort in this love, because it's real and never dies.

Pam is currently developing a series of programs with other volunteers to support the spouses of terminally ill cancer patients. Pam, who lives in Chaska, Minnesota, and works in the insurance industry, says that Fanny and Chester, two wonderful bull terriers, make her smile every day. In her story, she has an angel animal vision.

Our Beloved Dog Appeared to Reassure Me

Pam Fine

On a brutal winter morning in 1987, my dog, Buddy, died. I loved and grieved for him as much as, and quite possibly more than, I had for my own dear parents.

Buddy, at 125 pounds, weighed more than I do. He stood a head taller than me when he put his big paws on my shoulders and licked me on my arrival home from work each night. Big as he was in stature, Buddy's heart and gentle nature were even bigger.

Each morning, before my husband and I awoke, Buddy would ever so carefully climb up on the pillows above our heads. When the alarm sounded, he was our official greeter for each day.

The love and joy that this wonderful creature brought to our family is impossible to measure. But it is what happened after his death that is truly incredible.

Buddy Appeared to Me After He Died

In the more than ten years since that devastating November morning when Buddy died, I've actually seen him twice. Both times, he heralded things to come and delivered a message of bad news, yet his appearance gave me tremendous reassurance.

Before my husband was diagnosed with non-Hodgkin's lymphoma, Buddy came to see me. Though I was in my bedroom, I wasn't asleep. It may be hard to believe, but I actually saw Buddy. This vision was accompanied by a very warm feeling that comforted me as if I were being wrapped in a blanket of love. At the time, I simply thought Buddy had returned to let me know that he was okay. It wasn't until years later that I finally realized why he had visited me. This understanding came to me gradually, after his next appearance.

The second time I saw Buddy was early on a mist-filled morning, almost five years later. I stepped to the front window of my house to see how thick the fog was outside. In the mist, I saw my beautiful Buddy. Our contact was brief but very powerful. Then he was gone. From his visit, I clearly understood that something was coming into my life that would involve tremendous heartbreak. Yet, Buddy's message to me was that I'd have the strength to heal.

One week after I saw Buddy in the mist, my only daughter was diagnosed with Hodgkin's disease.

As I write this story, it's been six months since I saw Buddy. During that period, my husband died and my daughter finished her treatment. We await the results of tests to confirm that she's in remission.

There are many cultures in our world that believe animals are our spiritual links. From my own experience, I know that Buddy is mine. When he comes to me again, I'll be sure that, whatever lessons are in my path, I'll be able to walk through them to the other side.

> **A Tail to Wag:** Are angel animals spiritual links for us? Is an angel animal who has passed over to the other side still bringing you love and spiritual comfort? Do angel animals let us know that we're never alone or forgotten?

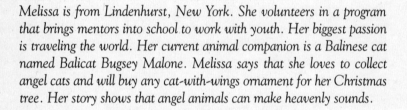

Melissa is from Lindenhurst, New York. She volunteers in a program that brings mentors into school to work with youth. Her biggest passion is traveling the world. Her current animal companion is a Balinese cat named Balicat Bugsey Malone. Melissa says that she loves to collect angel cats and will buy any cat-with-wings ornament for her Christmas tree. Her story shows that angel animals can make heavenly sounds.

The Heavenly Meow

Melissa Gentile

On my twenty-sixth birthday, Sashie found me. I'd never had a cat before and was reluctant to be adopted by one. My sister called me while I was in Italy and said that a beautiful kitten was standing outside her door. She had the feeling that this kitty would be just right for me.

When I arrived home, a friendly blue kitten leaped into my arms and my life. My mother didn't want to keep him, but after a clean bill of health and an adorable show that won her heart, Sashie was accepted as the newest member of my family.

During the next year, Sashie brought love and laughter to everyone. He had a permanent smile on his face that made people smile back at him. Sashie's crazy antics included watching television and chasing the characters to the back of the set. He ran, jumped, and played in his kitty paradise. Every morning, at 5:00, he'd gently knock on the door to remind someone to feed him. Each evening, as we walked in the door, Sashie was always there to greet us.

In September 1995, his antics started to slow down. I thought he was just becoming more mature but I was wrong. In the months to follow, Sashie developed arthritis and behavior problems. A vet, who never gave up hope, treated the cat for months for an increasing number of problems.

Finally, after he had stayed for two nights at the vet, I brought Sashie home. Within two days, he went totally blind. My vet searched the country for a specialist who could help. The only advice this consultant could give was to put Sashie to sleep.

Sashie Went to Kitty Heaven

Sashie went to kitty heaven on February 4, 1996. He was only one and a half years old. My immediate family and cousins all came with me to the vet to say good-bye. I wrapped Sashie in his blanket because the only sense he had left was touch. I didn't want him to feel the cold steel table beneath him. The vet cried along with us as Sashie left. I truly think it hurt him as much as it did me. We stayed there until after we knew Sashie was gone.

I returned home that day with a heavy heart, not thinking that I'd ever feel better. However, I found comfort in many ways. On the day after we'd lost Sashie, flowers arrived at my house with a card that read, "I'm home. I love you, Sashie."

Later, a stranger sent me the story of the Rainbow Bridge, an anonymously written story that is often passed from person to person and comforts people who have lost pets. The story reassured me that Sashie's spirit lived on. It helped when a friend of the family told me about Saint Francis of Assisi and his love for animals. I prayed every night and asked Saint Francis to comfort Sashie.

But one more remarkable incident helped me and my family through our grieving over Sashie.

During the week of Sashie's death, all of my family members heard a faint mew from an area of the house that has no window or way for an animal to be in it. I didn't believe their stories until I went to the room to listen for the sound. When I arrived at the room, we all heard, "Meow!" I cried. I raced outside to check for tracks in the newly fallen snow. There were none. I heard the mewing sound again later that night when I was alone.

I believe that my beloved Sashie was saying to me, "I'm home. I love you, Sashie."

A Paw to Lick: Is sound another way that angel animals let us know that there is a heaven and they are in it? Could you comfort someone who is grieving over the loss of a beloved friend by sharing Sashie's story?

Gwen is from Howell, New Jersey. She raises and shows quarter horses. Gwen also has a golden retriever, Brittany; an aged gelding, Jesse; a mare, Charm; and Charm's daughter, Easter. Gwen says that if she accomplishes nothing else in her life, she'd be happy just to know that the world is a better, safer place for all animals, especially dogs and horses. Her story of angel animal horses reminds us that there are many ways to receive signs from God when we're faced with tough choices.

Rusty's Colt Let Us Know His Mother Could Finally Join Him

Gwen Ajar

Rusty Miss, a liver-colored chestnut mare, was an animal companion for my daughter. Rusty had a foal, Stormy Mac, who died when he was only seven years old. Sadly, this beautiful creature's promising future was cut short when he died in the early morning on September 29, the day after my daughter's birthday.

As she grew older, Rusty became more arthritic. Although we could no longer ride her, my daughter kept the horse as a companion. But after watching Rusty's pain increase over the months to a point where we could no longer manage it with drugs, we agonized over the decision of whether or not to put her to sleep. One spring morning, as I walked out the back door toward the barn, I heard a horse whinny from the left side of my house. There are no paddock areas near the house, so I thought that a horse had somehow gotten loose during the night. I immediately ran to the barn to find out what had happened.

When I got to the barn, I found all the horses where they

belonged. Then I heard another whinny. I turned back to look and caught a glimpse of movement in the trees. I recognized the familiar whinny. It was Rusty's colt, Stormy. This same colt had appeared to me in fleeting glimpses after his death. That's how I could be so certain that it was Stormy visiting me again.

Had Stormy somehow sensed our indecision about letting go of Rusty? Seeing a vision of him in the trees made me realize that Rusty's colt had come to let us know that it would be all right if we decided to have his mother put to sleep. And he was here to take the journey with her.

We made our decision that day. Although it was a very sad time for us, there was a measure of comfort in knowing that Rusty wasn't alone. She'd be joining her colt, Stormy.

We Commemorated the Two Horses

After Rusty's death, we made a donation for planting an oak tree at the horse park near our home. This place is deeded for eternity with no chance of the land being developed. Coincidentally, the dedication ceremony had been postponed from an August date to September 28, the day of my daughter's birthday. Before the ceremony, I walked the grounds to find the trees that had been planted in Rusty's and Stormy's memory. I found the plaque and read the inscription. As incredible as it may sound, in the midst of a crystal blue sky, a dark cloud formed, and the wind began to blow strongly enough to push me off balance.

Now, I know very well that there could be a logical explanation for this strange weather. But, somehow, I feel more at ease and choose to believe that although Rusty and Stormy are gone, these exceptional creatures, who were so much a part of our lives, still communicate with us.

A Tail to Swish: Do angel animals, in heaven and on earth, play important roles by delivering spiritual messages? Could an angel animal be trying to help when you're faced with a tough decision?

Debi, a legal secretary for the Washington state attorney general's office, lives in Lacey, Washington. She loves cats and belongs to several cat organizations. Debi's special animal companions are two cousins, Moki, a sable Burmese male, and Jazzy, a true Bombay female, who is all black with big gold eyes. Her angel animal, Missey Kitten, offers the message that life is a precious gift.

My Cat Called Me Back to Life

Debi Reimann

Was suicide such a hard reality when my life was filled with so much pain and unhappiness? Severely depressed and confused, I didn't know which way to turn. Estranged from family and friends, I felt that positively nobody cared about me. Death beckoned appealingly. All I had to do was just take pills and go to sleep. I'd never again have to face pain and uncertainty.

One night I decided only one more drink and a few pills would bring me to a point where no one would ever hurt me again. I felt myself sliding into a wonderful sleep that would soon release me from all my misery. The life I no longer cared to live would end.

Although my body slept, I felt myself floating through a gray mist. Flooded with joy, I had a sense of traveling into a tunnel of light. The sensation of intense love flowed through me, creating waves of happiness and peace. Compassion and understanding were all around. Everything was so lovely and beautiful. I was safe at last. The pain was gone.

A Vision Appeared in Front of Me

Then a vision formed in front of me. This being appeared to be as wise and old as the ages, but his message was not what I wanted to hear. The vision gently told me I couldn't stay. He said that it wasn't my time yet. His loving touch was like nothing I'd ever known or imagined. The absolute serenity I experienced while in his presence will remain with me always.

I knew that death would be a new beginning. I didn't want to return to the pain-racked existence that was my life. I longed to stay in the light and feel this peace engulf me. But as the vision tenderly guided me back through the tunnel of light, he reassured me that someday I'd return to this bliss.

Then, at the end of the tunnel, I saw my precious Missey Kitten. He was calling me back.

I turned and asked the vision why there was so much pain and anguish in my life. He smiled and told me that, sometimes, in order to comprehend genuine happiness and tranquillity, we must first endure the darkest realms of our consciousness.

Later, in my lonely hospital bed, I thought about what the vision had said and knew I had to let go of bitterness to discover the harmony and joy I so desperately sought. As I reflected on this experience, I knew that death was nothing to fear. I am immortal and indestructible. I have always existed and would continue to do so. I'd seen my own wonderfulness and gentleness. My life's reality was full of love and goodness, if I would only give it a chance.

After my failed attempt at suicide, I had to forgive myself and learn that life is full of errors and lessons. I'd made an error. But I'd also learned the important lessons that life is precious and

that I'm not alone. I knew that there is no pain too great to survive and no unhappiness I can't change.

Just as Missey had been waiting for me to return to him
through the tunnel between life and death, this wonderful cat
helped me through the next difficult months as I faced my problems and began to live life anew.

When Missey died, I felt alone and empty once again.

Missey Returned to Help Me Live

One spring day, the year after Missey died, I sat at a traffic
light and heard a soft purr. I looked over and there sat Missey.
The moment that he appeared to me saved my life. A drunk
driver had just run the red light. If I'd started driving when the
light turned green, instead of looking at Missey, my life would
have ended.

There are times when my life becomes frightening and unsure,
but after these spiritual experiences, I now know there is a sacred
place deep within to which I can return to become rejuvenated
and feel unconditional love.

I know that I don't need to retaliate against people who have
hurt me. I've found that very little in life is worth getting upset
about. I've regained my lightheartedness, serenity, and inner
peace. I realize that everything is unfolding as it should. But the
best part of all is knowing that my Missey Kitten will be there to
meet me in heaven when my time comes to go there. Until then,
I will always have a kitty in my life, because these animals are my
connection to unconditional love and inner peace.

Missey taught me these spiritual lessons in his own sweet way.

A Paw to Lick: What sweet lessons are angel animals teaching you? Do angel animals return from heaven to help us realize
how blessed each moment of life is?

Allen's story relates his own experience with an angel animal who brought an important message of life after death.

An Angel Animal's Dream

ALLEN ANDERSON

Two years before we moved to Minnesota, we visited a family who had a litter of golden retriever pups. Our children were nearing their teenage years, my wife, Linda, and I both had stressful jobs, and we were looking for an addition to our family who would bring more unconditional love into our home.

All of the puppies were so cute that we couldn't decide which one to choose. Linda playfully told the group of puppies, "One of you is going to have to choose us." Without hesitation, one of the pups came to me and untied my shoestrings. So, we asked the pup if she wanted to go home with us. She responded by following us as we walked away, leaving her littermates behind.

We asked this puppy what she wanted to be called. Immediately, the unusual name Prana came to Linda's mind. Later we looked up the meaning of this word and found that its definition was "breath of life." And that is what this little puppy became for our family. She taught us all how to relax, love, and breathe in the fullness of life.

Prana Loved Visiting a Sacred Temple's Grounds

A few years after Prana adopted us, we moved to Minneapolis, Minnesota. Part of my new job there was keeping a beautiful temple open after regular office hours for visitors and social events. The building was situated in the middle of a rolling prairie. I'd take Prana to work with me each evening. With all her heart, she loved this place and seemed to sense its sacredness. When there was no chance of her bothering visitors, I'd take her off the leash, so she could run with her ears flapping in the wind through the grassy, rolling prairie hills.

One weekend, Linda and I discussed our observations that Prana wasn't looking as healthy as she'd always been. We'd both noticed that Prana was sleeping more and had less energy. We took her to the vet, and when he X-rayed her, he found an obstruction that could be cancerous. Prana would need to have an operation.

With her surgery looming the next day, I took Prana to the temple grounds that she most loved to visit. I parked the car and let her out. She was as excited with anticipation as usual, but this night, it broke my heart to watch her jump out of the car, hit the pavement, and squeal in pain. Prana looked at me, then she tried to run. She could only go a short distance into the prairie. Soon, she walked back to me with her head lowered. I bent down, hugged her, and cried. Quietly, I stood near her as she looked around and quietly said good-bye to her special place.

I helped her get into the front seat of the car and we drove away. On every other trip to the temple, Prana had always looked back at the prairie as we left it. This time, though, she looked straight ahead. There was nothing either one of us could do to change the fact that this would probably be her last visit.

The Vet Called with News About Prana's Condition

The next day, while Prana lay motionless on the operating table, the vet called us with devastating news. Prana had advanced cancer. It was so invasive that the best choice would be for her not to be awakened.

By then, everyone at the vet's office had grown attached to our little love angel. The staff often commented on what a special dog Prana was. The vet's voice broke when he told me the sad news. He later said that Prana's case had been very unusual. Apparently, Prana tried so hard to stay alive that her intestine wall had started to grow new healthy tissue around one of the tumors. But the cancer had already taken too heavy a toll on her body and she couldn't heal.

We weren't the only ones, though, who suffered from losing Prana. About a year before Prana's death, we'd gotten a new kitten and named him Feisty. Before Prana died, she raised Feisty as a well-behaved dog, letting him eat her food, showing him how to greet us at the door, and teaching him other uncatlike things to do in our family. The loss of Prana was heart-wrenching for all of us. We were amazed at how empty we felt without her in our lives. But Feisty mourned for his big sister most of all. For hours, he'd sit at the window looking, waiting for her to return.

It Was Time to Open Our Hearts to Another Dog

Two years after Prana died, Linda and I decided that we were finally ready to adopt another puppy. We knew no one could replace Prana, but we felt that our family needed the special brand of unconditional love that only a puppy can deliver. A puppy would also be a companion for Feisty.

The night before we were to look at some yellow Lab puppies, I had a wonderful dream.

Prana and I are walking on an ocean beachfront. It feels so wonderful to be with her again. I've missed her very much. Looking at her in this dream makes me feel better. She was such an important part of my life. I'm filled with happiness and joy at being with this beloved angel.

Suddenly, Prana jumps into the ocean's surf and gently picks up a puppy by the skin of the neck. She carries the little creature to me, gently placing the yellow and tan puppy at my feet. The pup is small, cute, and playful.

The next day Linda and I went to see a farmer who had Labrador retriever puppies. Once again, we were faced with choosing from a litter of adorable puppies. Suddenly, one of the pups came over to me and untied my shoelaces. I looked down and recognized her as the yellow-tan pup Prana had delivered to my feet in the dream the previous night. I knew that with this untied shoelace, Prana's way of choosing us years ago, the pup was telling us that she would be our new companion. And she'd been personally chosen by Prana.

We named the dog Taylor, as a play on words, because her tail wagged so much it would make her fall over at times. The first few weeks Taylor was with us, she seemed to be following Prana's instructions and doing whatever would be necessary to fit into the family.

From these experiences with Prana, I learned that the spiritual, loving connections our beloved animal companions make with us never end.

A Tail to Wag: Could an angel animal appear in your dreams to help you make choices? Are angel animals bringing messages from heaven, through dreams and in other ways, that we ignore because we don't realize their significance?

More Messages from Heaven

Perhaps Jan Snyder's story, "Kitty and Melvin's Message of Hope," will help to answer the question about whether animals go to heaven. Jan, a pet store owner from Minneapolis, Minnesota, writes that a high-speed, head-on collision with a drunken driver claimed her husband of twenty-three years. As a result of this accident, Jan's health and ability to take care of herself and her family diminished. At about this same time, her cat of twelve years, Kitty, died of crippling cancer.

Jan says, "I needed to know that God was taking good care of her soul. I asked for a positive sign."

One evening Jan went to bed and lay on her back. Her other cat, Melvin, promptly hopped onto the bed and rested on her chest, looking right into Jan's face and purring just as Kitty used to do. This was something seven-year-old Melvin had never done before. Jan writes, "Yes, little Kitty's soul was in good care."

The next chapter will introduce you to something you may have already discovered. Angel animals often return to us in mystical ways that defy human logic but comfort the heart.

Chapter Twelve

Recognizing Angel Animals
Who Return

With almost complete unanimity, animal communicators told me that past lives could be seen in the animals' minds, if the animals chose to show them, and many did, if asked.

—Arthur Myers

*I*s it possible that angel animals have more love in their hearts than they can give and receive in one short lifetime? Has the Creator devised a divine plan for the return of our angel animals as an act of mercy and compassion from a loving God? Do they come back to us as gifts wrapped in different packages?

Is it just an adage that cats have nine lives? Could angel animals make round-trips from one life to another? Has an angel animal used a return ticket to be with you?

These are questions you'll have to answer in your own heart. The stories in this chapter will give you thoughts to ponder as you contemplate some of the mysteries of life (or lives). We found them to be intriguing records of the mystical and miraculous ways angel animals return to those they left behind.

Bob is a flight operations manager for a major airline and a minister in his church in Spring, Texas. He's done public speaking throughout the United States and in South America. He and his wife, Suzanne, share their home with four cats—Oscar, Mitsu, Sasha, and Amber—Anamee, their puppy, as well as a flock of critters they feed in their backyard. Bob says that he's learned a lot about life and love from his animal companions. His story helps us recognize how angel animals can let us know that they are returning.

Thank God, Namo Returned to Us!

BOB HAYES

Namo, our beautiful dog, died two days after Hurricane Andrew demolished our family's home in Miami. Namo was a great protector of my wife, Suzanne, and our daughter. He was also very gentle with our cat family. Namo had the angelic characteristics of a very special soul. I sometimes feel that he left us in 1992 because he sensed that his spiritual assignment was complete.

About three months after Namo's death, I had a fascinating dream about him.

In the dream:

Namo appears as handsome as he looked before his death. But then the dog walks into a pool of water. When he emerges, he is a beautiful reddish color.

Was My Dream Prophetic?

A few days after my dream about Namo, some friends came to visit for a spiritual discussion class at our home. Two of the ladies in this group brought their dog, Flow Jo, a Hungarian breed vizsla. Their dog was a beautiful reddish color, the same shade as the dog I'd seen in my dream. The woman told us that Flow Jo was pregnant by another vizsla and she mentioned when Flow Jo's pups would be born. I began to wonder, *Had Namo returned as one of these pups? Was my dream prophetic?*

After Flow Jo had her puppies, Suzanne and I visited the litter. I asked for spiritual guidance to help me recognize if one of these puppies was Namo returning to me. The first puppy that the woman with the litter showed me was the littlest one, the runt. But this puppy seemed to be glowing as she held him in her hands.

She put the pup on the ground. He walked over and sat by my chair. The whole time I talked to the woman, the puppy's brothers and sisters romped around, chewing on my shoes, but this little fellow didn't budge. When I picked him up, he licked my face. Then, he stared at me for a long time and I just knew that our old friend and protector had returned. Even the lady selling the pups said, "He knows you."

We gave the puppy the name Anamee. One day, after bringing Anamee home, I contemplated this profound experience of having Namo come back to us. As I sat quietly, reflecting on what had happened, I could clearly see Anamee as a big, strong dog of about seventy-five pounds. I also could hear my wife saying, "Thank God, Namo returned to us!"

A Paw to Lick: Is it possible that angel animals are not only our best friends for life but for lives? Could your dreams predict that an angel animal has chosen to be with you again? Pull out your photo albums and compare photos of the angel animals who have befriended you—then and now—and look into their eyes.

Myron is an acupuncturist, a practitioner of Chinese medicine, a researcher, and inventor working in the fields of natural health and tai chi. Tuza and Ardas are two cats who live with Myron and his wife, Debbie, in Eden Prairie, Minnesota.

It's Not Once a Cat, Always a Cat

Myron Cheshaek

Wiki was really my sister's cat, but she adopted me. A sweet and loving grey cat, Wiki would have preferred to be indoors, but my parents changed their pet policy and all animals had to go outside. Before Wiki was delegated to the orchard, she used to snuggle with me at night. After she'd satisfied her cuddle quota, Wiki would retire to her self-appointed guard post at the end of my bed. I missed her when she was thrown out of the house and didn't like it that sometimes she was gone for days.

Years later, after I'd grown up and moved to Minneapolis, my parents were moving and sent Wiki to be with me. When she came to my home, she returned to the enjoyment of being an indoor cat—warm, cozy, and protected. Wiki happily spent her final years with me. Her only problem seemed to be that days before her passing, Wiki developed a muscle twitch.

A few years after Wiki died, my dreams, which I listen to, started telling me that I was going to be getting a new cat. Even though I already had another cat, I decided to start looking for this newcomer.

I went to many pet stores but couldn't find the right cat for me. The cats didn't seem to fit what I was looking for.

What *was* I looking for?

If you had asked me that question, I couldn't have answered it. None of the kittens I saw fit the image I had of the cat who was supposed to come home with me. I'd pick the kittens up, hold them, and look at them, but I just knew that they weren't right.

I Found the Kitten I'd Been Looking For

One day I was walking by a pet store and had a strong feeling that I should go in. I asked where the kittens were and was told that a half-dozen kitties had just arrived.

As soon as I turned the corner to the kitten area, I spotted *the one* immediately. I knew that he was the kitten I'd been looking for. As I walked toward him, a woman who was there before me picked him up.

I thought, *Oh no! Please put him down!*

Deciding to be patient, I walked around the store and came back. I waited to see what would happen, hoping that this woman wouldn't take my kitten. If she did, I'd have to speak with her, because I simply wasn't willing to give him up. I walked back over to play with the other kittens and to be sure that I was near in case the woman didn't want the kitten I had to have. Finally, she put him down. Immediately I took the kitten to the counter to adopt him.

The kitten and I instantly bonded as I drove him home. I named him Ardas.

Almost immediately, Ardas began to remind me of Wiki. He liked being an indoor cat, but even when he was a kitten, he had very mature outdoor skills. When I took Ardas outside, he'd find cover and hide, only coming out when he was sure it was safe. He somehow already knew how to be careful outdoors. I wondered, *Could Wiki have somehow come back into my life?*

Ardas's coloring was the same as Wiki's grey coat, and he loved to cuddle with me at night, then retire to the end of the bed to guard me, just as Wiki had. Also, similar to Wiki, he didn't like playing alone but enjoyed it more when I invented ways to entertain him.

I think when Ardas's muscles started to twitch as Wiki's had toward the end of her life, I finally realized that my old companion Wiki was back in a new kitty's physical body. And we could all be a family again.

The Life of a Dog

I was about to have an even greater surprise about how animals return for other rounds of life on earth. Wiki had been totally catlike and out of his love came back to be with me again. But as Ardas developed a new personality in this life, he showed signs that he hadn't always lived as a cat.

When Ardas was a kitten, he used to play fetch, catching whatever I threw to him and bringing his toy back to be thrown again. Now, when my wife, Debbie, and I return home after being gone for a long time, Ardas rolls over on his back waiting for his tummy to be rubbed. In addition to having been my cat, Wiki, we wondered if Ardas could have been a dog in yet another past life!

On the way home from the vet one very warm day, Ardas rode with his head hanging out the window, panting, with his tongue out. We remembered that all the way on the long truck ride when we were moving from Portland to Minneapolis, Ardas hung his head out the window, tongue first.

We started thinking about the things Ardas does that we've never seen cats do. For example, he lies on the floor with his back legs sprawled out behind him and he comes when you call, "Ardas!" How many cats do you know who scratch on the door when they want to go out? Ardas does.

Yes, we've concluded, Ardas, aka Wiki, probably at some time used to be a dog. And we have the pure joy of watching his hilarious dog act in a cat's body.

A Paw to Lick: How many lives do you think angel animal cats have? And could they spend some of them as dogs? Have you ever had the impression that an angel animal has returned to you? Now that you've read Myron's story, observe the angel animals in your life to see if they've returned in imaginative ways.

Beverly is affiliated with the ministry of a foundation that offers services to individuals on their path to enlightenment. Beverly has been married to her husband, Paul, for thirty-nine years. She has two married daughters and one granddaughter. At home in Double Oak, Texas, Beverly has two "shadows" who are her constant companions—Beau, a miniature red poodle, and Joey, a silver-grey toy poodle. Beverly's story about Joey offers a startling glimpse at the possibility that angel animals can prepare us for their return.

Angels Returning in Disguise

Beverly Hale Watson

"This is Officer Dewicki. Your daughter, Kim has been injured in an automobile accident. She's being transported to the hospital downtown. Can you or your husband please report to the emergency room as soon as possible?"

Shaken by the officer's message, I quickly hung up the phone, located my husband, Paul, and told him what had happened. We decided he'd go to the hospital, since my parents were scheduled to arrive at the house any moment from out of state. Not five minutes before the phone rang, I had looked at the kitchen clock and made the comment, "I think something has happened. Kim is very punctual and should have been home by now."

Hospital-bound, my husband could see police officers directing traffic at a main intersection within five minutes of our home. As he came closer to the scene, he noticed our car sandwiched between two vehicles. Rammed from behind so hard, it had crashed into the rear end of the car in front. The impact left our car looking like an accordion on both ends. People were still being loaded into ambulances as Paul approached one of the police officers and identified himself.

Officer Dewicki explained that the emergency vehicle carrying Kim had just departed for the hospital. She'd suffered multiple injuries, but he felt they weren't life-threatening. "A higher power certainly was watching over her," he said. Paul thanked the police for their help and hurried to the hospital.

Upon his arrival, Kim had already been X-rayed and seen by a doctor. Hours later, she was released from the hospital wearing a neck brace and carrying pain killer prescriptions. We didn't know that this would be the beginning of a yearlong recovery period.

We Needed Help with Kim's Recovery

Kim required twenty-four-hour care. As days became weeks and weeks became months, the strain from this situation took its toll on all of us. For Kim, the accident had created severe problems in the muscles that had absorbed the impact of the crash. Her neck and head injuries caused dizziness, double vision, headaches, and limited mobility. This was compounded by her intermittent drug reactions, which created additional stress and frustration. As time wore on, she became very depressed.

Looking at alternatives for bringing Kim out of her emotional slump, we decided to get a miniature poodle puppy. Toby came to our home at eight weeks of age. He was a little black ball of fluff, just full of life. He bonded with Kim immediately. With the pup as her responsibility, we knew that Kim would become functional.

In the following months, Kim and Toby were inseparable. Often I'd watch as they walked down the street. Kim would be talking to Toby and he'd look intently at her as if in total understanding. He seemed to have a sixth sense. Toby knew when Kim was having bad days. During these times, he'd very gently climb up next to her on the sofa or bed and lie for hours at her side. Other times, he'd give Kim a few licks on the arm as if to say, "I'm here for you." At night, Toby would lie where he could see both of our bedrooms. If Kim rustled in her bed, he'd get up to check on her. If he felt something was wrong, he'd get me, then wait until I followed him into her room.

Toby became a master at communicating with us. I often commented, "I don't think this dog knows he's a dog; he thinks he's a person." There was no doubt in our minds that this animal was special. His unending love and devotion to our daughter contributed greatly to her recovery as she battled numerous physical setbacks and bouts of depression. One year after the accident, Kim returned to college, leaving Toby in my care.

Toby Told Me His Secrets

For the next eleven years Toby was my constant companion. Then, one day when I returned home, I noticed that only half of Toby's body was functioning. I thought that he'd probably had a stroke. Paul picked him up and we left immediately for the veterinary hospital. After four hours of testing, it was determined that the dog's spine was disintegrating. Vertebrae had rammed together, making it impossible for him to move two of his legs, and there was pressure on his neck. The doctor suggested we take Toby home and decide what we wanted to do about his condition.

Later that day, I held Toby in my arms. To my surprise, I

started receiving telepathic thoughts from him. At first I thought it was my imagination. But the messages continued, and I definitely knew they weren't my thoughts. Toby asked if I'd get a huge cushion and set it on an angle, leaning it against the sofa. Lying on a slant took pressure off his neck and caused less pain than if he were flat on the floor. He also asked if I would put his water and food bowls on the small step stool since he couldn't bend his head downward. And last, he wanted to know if I'd please stay with him that night.

I can't express in words what I felt after unmistakable communication with Toby. It was unbelievable!

Of course, I complied with his requests. During the night, we decided we'd release Toby back to God, for he'd only been sent to us on loan. The next morning, we returned to the veterinarian's office. When we set Toby on the floor, he had recovered from his previous paralysis and moved all four legs. He walked in continuous circles, his tail wagging. The expression on his face conveyed a happy message—Toby knew that he was returning to his heavenly home. Through our tears, Paul and I said good-bye and left him behind.

As I opened the car door, Toby once again started conversing telepathically. "I'm free! I'm free!" he conveyed to me. He told me that I should envision him as a lamb leaping over clouds, no longer in pain. Then he said, "One day you're going to receive a phone call from a woman who is moving out of state. She'll have a one-year-old silver-grey poodle and she can't take the dog with her. She'll ask if you'll take him and give him a home. You'll say, 'Yes.' When this happens, I'll be returning."

Toby's Return

The following March, as I stood in the kitchen washing dishes, the phone rang. When I answered it, a woman said, "I just finished talking to someone at the Humane Society. She said that you have a daughter who volunteers there, and gave me your name. I'm moving to South Carolina. I have a one-year-old silver-grey toy poodle who needs a home. I can't take him with me. I know you're supposed to have him, but I don't know why. Can you come over to the house tonight and pick up Joey?"

Absolutely dumbfounded by what this stranger had just said, I quickly tried to regain my composure and agreed to meet her. I called Paul right away to tell him about the phone call. The two of us were in total disbelief.

That evening, we went to meet Joey.

When we entered the woman's home, Paul sat on her sofa. Joey jumped into his lap and wasn't about to leave. Within one hour, the woman told us about Joey's habits, likes, and dislikes. She gave us copies of his shot records, birth certificate, and licenses. She seemed totally relieved that Joey was going to a good home where he'd be loved and well cared for.

When we came home, Paul took Joey inside and put him on the front foyer floor. Joey looked around for a couple of minutes, then headed up the stairs to our bedroom. Within minutes, he leaped on our bed and tunneled under the comforter to the foot of the bed where Toby used to sleep. Then Joey jumped to the floor and started running through the house. We watched in amazement. His movements were identical to Toby's. When the dog finally started settling down, we put him outside in the back-yard. All of a sudden Joey started running. We couldn't believe what we saw. He looked like a lamb leaping over clouds, just as Toby had described the way I should envision him leaving this earth.

There was no doubt in our minds. Toby had indeed returned.

It's said that God can send messengers—angels—in many forms. Sometimes they appear as human beings, birds, butterflies, or other animals. Toby came to our home in our hour of need. He brought us great love, compassion, and enjoyment. With his illness and death, he awakened my inner senses to a world beyond. Then, he returned as he'd foretold, wearing a silver-grey coat, sporting four-on-the-floor, and leaping like a lamb.

Is he a dog? Or is he an angel returning in disguise?

A Tail to Wag: Could angel animals return to us? Is it possible that, as part of a divine plan, angel animals come back to give and receive more love?

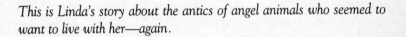

This is Linda's story about the antics of angel animals who seemed to want to live with her—again.

The Mugsie/Feisty Duo Doubled My Pleasure and Fun

LINDA ANDERSON

Before I got married, my cat, Mugsie, shared my apartment. After I brought him home from an animal shelter, he decided that I was his private property. When he saw me going through the rituals of preparing to go out for the evening, Mugsie communicated his displeasure. He'd lodge himself under my dressing table and stretch his paw in between the gaps in the curtain tacked around the edge of the table. Then, he'd swipe at my hand while I tried to apply my makeup. If that didn't distract me enough, Mugsie would leap to the light switch and flip it off.

After I became familiar with his routine, I learned to continue while Mugsie launched the next phase of attack. He'd plop his rear end on the top button of the radio to turn it on and push the knob, making it play louder. All of these shenanigans usually didn't stop me, so he'd start nibbling on the plants.

That worked.

I'd chase him out of the room, much to his obvious delight.

Mugsie was an angel animal who found ways to make sure I got his messages. Once I unwrapped a birthday present on my coffee table, but the shiny, pink bow had fallen to the floor. The next day when I arrived home from work, Mugsie had carefully placed the bow on top of his leavings in the kitty litter box.

A present?

I wondered if he could have deliberately placed this bow in such a strategic position. I picked up the bow and put it back on the floor by the coffee table. The next evening, I returned from work to find the present on top of Mugsie's leavings again.

Were these the remains of the day?

Mugsie was communicating with me in his own inimitable fashion to let me know his opinion about being left home alone for too long. He thought it was a "poop-y" thing to do!

Once I sat in a chair wondering what Mugsie did to earn his keep. I thought about how I fed him, emptied his kitty litter, and took care of all his needs. What did he do for me? At this moment, as I questioned the balance between us, Mugsie high-stepped into the room. He walked over to the corner and wiped a cobweb off the wall. Then he turned and gave me a look that let me know I should never question his value again.

I didn't.

Mugsie Had More to Do Than He Could Finish

Mugsie lived to be twenty-one years old, seeing me through a divorce, a new marriage to Allen, and a move to the cold land of Minnesota. Finally, it was time for his rascally old body to give out. And, the cat who loved only me left this earth while I held him in my arms and cried. But before Mugsie left, he'd started living with our newest addition to the angel animal family, Prana, our gentle golden retriever. Prana tried everything to get Mugsie to accept her love. But the old critter consistently spurned the dog's affection.

Mugsie died never knowing how much more love he could have had.

The night before Mugsie left us, I promised him that if he ever wanted to return, I'd love to have him live with me again. I told him that he'd have to let me know he was back and how to find him. For I believe that cats have at least nine lives.

One afternoon, three years after Mugsie's passing, I took a nap and woke up with the sure knowledge that Mugsie had returned. I hurried to tell Allen that I couldn't explain it, but I just knew we had to get to the Humane Society immediately, because Mugsie would be there. Allen has all the qualities on my husband wish list, and one thing I especially appreciate about him is that, when I tell him something as crazy as this, he doesn't argue with me about it. I guess he's learned better over the years. So he drove me to the animal shelter and we started the frantic search for Mugsie with the anxiety that the building would be closing in thirty minutes.

Allen sat on the bench, probably trying to pretend he didn't know me, as I went from kitten to kitten asking, "Are you Mugsie?" I found a darling Russian blue kitten with velvety gray hair and took him to one of the visiting rooms. The kitten completely ignored me, turning his head from side to side to keep from looking at me. This was something Mugsie had always done when I'd left him for a while. But I admonished the kitten-who-could-be-Mugsie, "You left me. I didn't leave you." I couldn't get anywhere with him, but something was resonating inside of me. I just had a feeling this kitten was my beloved friend.

A family came to the room where I held the unfriendly cat. The mother said that they'd seen this kitten first and wanted him. Since he still wouldn't look at me, I handed him to her, thinking maybe I'd made a mistake. I went out to look at more kitties with only fifteen minutes now before closing. A few moments later, the woman called to me and asked if I wanted the kitten. She said that he didn't seem to like children and had hissed at her daughter.

I ran to grab him. *This has to be Mugsie!* I thought. He hadn't even been fond of my own children, because he didn't like sharing me with them. This time, the kitten crawled all over me. He licked and kissed me. He hurled his body against my heart and purred. I guess he knew that he'd almost lost his chance to come home. Allen and I hurried to the counter to adopt him—again.

Mugsie Let Us Know That He Remembered

When we brought the kitten home, he immediately began inspecting the house as if he were making certain that nothing had changed in his absence. One of the first acts was to hiss at Prana and appear disappointed that she was still around. To our surprise, this tiny kitten then ran to the door that opened to the second story of our house. He climbed up the stairs. When he arrived at the top, with all his strength, he clawed his way up onto the rocking chair that had been Mugsie's favorite spot and sat on the pillow, looking at us as if to say, "I'm back!"

We have many windows in our home. The kitten immediately found Mugsie's favorite window. Again, with great effort, he made it to the ledge and perched there, looking out over the backyard as Mugsie had done every day. He was definitely reclaiming his territory.

Over the next few weeks, we watched as the personality of Mugsie faded, and the new kitty, whom we named Feisty, emerged. Prana began to win him over with her gentle ways. Their bowls side by side, Prana always waited until the kitten ate before she'd touch her food. She licked, played, and slept curled up with the kitty. Soon, the two became the best of pals. Finally, he was able to accept the love that, as Mugsie, he'd rejected.

Then Prana began to raise Feisty to be a dog. He imitated everything she did, including the uncatlike behavior of running to the door, tail wagging, to greet us when we came home. We kept saying, "Feisty, you're a cat. You're supposed to be aloof." But he seemed to enjoy this new opportunity to love more freely.

Feisty grew into a most loving, affectionate cat. Nothing perturbed him. He didn't flinch at sudden noises, just turned his head slowly to see if he should get out of the way. Even visitors to our home commented on what a bundle of pure love he was in a cat's body. He was definitely an old soul who had seen and done it all.

From the Mugsie/Feisty duo, we learned that there's a very good reason for angel animals to return to this classroom we call life on earth. If they didn't or couldn't learn how to give and receive love the first, or the fiftieth, time around, it's worth trying again. And, besides, there are those humans who still can't seem to live very well without them.

A Paw to Lick: Has this story caused you to look at angel animals to see if they've been with you before? Is there an angel animal you remember from your childhood? Would you want to make a list of his or her personality traits? Compare these behaviors and characteristics with those of an angel animal who is in your life today.

What Have the Angel Animals Taught You?

Do angel animals find a way to return to the ones they love? When you adopt an angel animal, look into his or her eyes and decide for yourself if you see a familiar glow of love in them.

If you feel as we did after writing and researching this book, you may be realizing that you have a lot to think about now. Angel animals don't say much. They can't express their connection with the Divine in written words or language. But we hope that you've heard them in your heart. After all, that's where angels meet us, isn't it? In our hearts, our imaginations, and our souls.

May angel animals—messengers who assure us that God loves us unconditionally—protect and inspire you. And when angel animals grace your life, may you recognize and appreciate them.

More About Allen and Linda Anderson and Angel Animals

Allen and Linda Anderson are writers and inspirational speakers. Married since 1983, they share their home in Minneapolis with a menagerie of pets and volunteer at a local animal shelter. Linda has won national awards for her plays and short stories. She's traveled throughout the world and done hundreds of media interviews. Her previous book is *35 Golden Keys to Who You Are & Why You're Here*. Allen writes screenplays, articles, and fiction. He has a degree in journalism and was a reporter before he worked as a police officer in Atlanta for eight years. His photos and articles have been featured in regional and national publications.

Allen and Linda Anderson donate a portion of revenue from Angel Animals projects to animal shelters and organizations.

Here are ways to have more Angel Animals in your life:

- subscribe to *Angel Animals*, a bimonthly newsletter with inspiring stories, poems, and articles about how animals help people in amazing and miraculous ways
- submit stories and poems for future books and newsletters
- schedule an Angel Animals workshop or presentation to

discover how spiritually connecting with animals makes you healthier, wealthier, and wiser
• look for Angel Animals toys from Safari, Ltd. in toy stores and bookstores and on the Internet

Contact Allen and Linda Anderson at:

Angel Animals
P.O. Box 26488
Minneapolis, MN 55426
Web site: www.angelanimals.com

More About the Authors

Part One: What Angel Animals Teach Us About Relationships

Chapter One: *Discovering Your Spiritual Connection with All Life*

Chapter Two: Learning How to Love Unconditionally

Chapter Three: Creating Family Harmony

© 1997, Kristin von Kreisler, *The Compassion of Animals: True Stories of Animal Courage and Kindness*, Prima Publishing, 3875 Atherton Road, Rocklin, CA 95765, www.primapublishing.com. Reprinted with permission.

© 1998, Peter Lucchese, "Pal, a Member of the Family."

© 1998, Patricia Fish, "Bird Children."

© 1998, Kristy Walker, "Misha, the Good Daddy Cat."

© 1998, Deborah Wolusky, "How a Cat Helped me Cope with First-Time Parenthood."

© 1998, Kellie Sisson Snider, "Two Birds Taught Remorse and Forgiveness."

© 1998, Sally A. Voelske, "The Family of Miracle Workers."

© 1998, Michael Abbott, "The Raccoons Adopted Me."

© 1998, Carol Frysinger, "A Family with Fluffy Love." Carol asks for women volunteers who want to help with her *Finding Mr. Right* book research. Contact her by E-mail at cafrys@yahoo.com.

© 1998, Janice M. Waddleton, "How Joe, the Cat, Got a Couch of His Own." Janice's work has been published in the journal *Sistersong: Women Across Cultures*, Vol. 4, No. 1.

© 1998, Sue Cassidy, "Pepper, a Family Dog."

© 1998, Teri Olcott, "Ninja Makes Sure I Eat Breakfast."

Chapter Four: Being Inspired to Pursue a Greater Good

© 1991, Gary Kowalski, *The Souls of Animals*, Stillpoint Publishing, Box 640, Meetinghouse Road, Walpole, NH 03608. Reprinted with permission.

© 1998, Glenna Moore, "Puss Puss Teaches How to Be an Angel."

© 1998, Lynn Duffey, "Bishop Answers a Call for Help."

© 1998, Allen Anderson, "Allen's Inspiration."

© 1998, Harry E. Oakes Jr., "My Work with the Search and Rescue Man." Harry E. Oakes Jr. runs the International K-9 Search and Rescue Services. You can contact Harry at P.O. Box 30364, Portland, OR 97230, call him at (503) 650-1904, or E-mail him at searchdog@cnnw.net.

© 1998, Bo Wise, "Henry, the Spider, Wove a Web of Creativity for Me." Bo publishes *The Shifting Times*, which she describes as a "newsmagazine for opening minds." It's circulated in the Cleveland/Akron/

Canton area of Ohio. Its mission is to offer the most up-to-date information in the fields of human potential, spiritual growth, and metaphysics. *The Shifting Times* offers syndicated columns and features stories about the spiritual paths of well-known actors, bestselling authors and lecturers, professional athletes, and more. For more information, call (330) 833-0451 or write to *The Shifting Times*, P.O. Box 289, Massillon, OH 44648.

© 1998, Kurt D. Welch, "The Deer Helped Me Win a College Scholarship."

© 1998, Linda Lansdell, " 'Throwaway' Kids and 'Throwaway' Animals Found Each Other."

© 1998, Judy Fay McLaughlin, "A Bird Helped Me Discover the Purpose of My Life."

© 1998, John Marikos, "A Dog and Cat Became Our Business Partners."

© 1998, Gretchen Youngdahl, "Migan Shows Me How to Be a Leader."

Part Two: What Angel Animals Teach Us About Handling Life's Challenges

© 1976, *Good News Bible, The Bible in Today's English Version*, under license from the American Bible Society, Thomas Nelson, Inc., Publishers, Nashville, TN.

Chapter Five: Sailing on the Winds of Change

© 1996, Sylvia Paine, "My Dog, Joe," *Mpls. St. Paul*, May 1996. Reprinted with permission of the author.

© 1998, Linda Anderson, "A Puppy Chooses a New Home."

© 1998, Linda Anderson, "The Woman Who Wanted a Barking Dog."

© 1997, Paul Revere Memorial Association by Patrick Leehey, *What Was the Name of Paul Revere's Horse? Twenty Questions about Paul Revere—Asked and Answered*, 19 North Square, Boston, MA 02113, (617) 523-2338.

© 1998, Julie Johnson Olson, "A Sparrow Led Me to Volunteer." Julie is the illustrator for this book. To talk to her about doing professional illustrations, call (800) 214-3860.

© 1998, Cheryl L. Yochim, "My Dog Taught Me How to Age Gracefully."

© 1998, Sally Rosenthal, "An Angel Without Wings Restored My

Spiritual Sight." Sally Rosenthal is a contributing editor to *Cats Magazine* and *LaJoie: The Journal in Appreciation of All Animals.* She's also a frequent contributor to other companion animal and disability rights magazines. Sally serves on the board of PetFriends, Inc., a national pet loss/bereavement hotline. E-mail her at beneman@aol.com.

© 1998, Rona Harding, "A Cat That Love Transformed."

© 1998, Jane L. Toleno, "Baxter Retires."

© 1998, M. E. Martucci, Ph.D., "Tanja's Secret Doorway to Freedom."

© 1998, Annie Holbrook, "Adversity Draws My Cat Family Together."

© 1998, Robin McBride, "Tomo Takes Charge of Change in His Life."

Chapter Six: Living Healthy

© 1998, Sharon Kunin, "Could It Be?"

© 1998, Jane Durst-Pulkys, "Simba Takes Away the Pain."

© 1998, Nancy Lucas Hampton, "Kringles's Healing Licks."

© 1998, Debbie Johnson, "A Kitty-Prescribed Solution." To order Debbie's books, *Think Yourself Thin* and *Think Yourself Loved,* or to invite her for a speaking engagement, call (800) 600-3483.

© 1998, Camille A. Lufkin, "A Rabbit's Cure for Migraine Headaches."

© 1998, David Leigh Litwin, "Pookie Taught Us How to Be Better Caretakers."

© 1998, Ann Archer, "The Dolphins Saved My Life."

© 1998, Anthony Taylor, "A Needy Cat Offered Me a Reason to Live."

© 1998, Kristy Walker, "Feeling Bad? Consult a Cat."

© 1998, Linda Anderson, "The Puppy and the Paralyzed Man."

Chapter Seven: Letting Go and Trusting

© 1995, Jelaluddin Rumi, "A Man and Woman Arguing," as quoted in *The Essential Rumi,* translated by Coleman Barks with John Moyne, A. J. Arbersy, and Reynold Nicholson, HarperSanFrancisco, a division of HarperCollins Publishers, 10 East 53rd Street, New York, NY 10022.

© 1998, Linda Anderson, "Communicating Doggie Adoption Tips."

© 1997, JoAnn M. Quintos, "Kuro Crossed the River of Hope."

© 1998, Victoria Bullis, "The Cat Who Knew How to Let Go of Pain." Victoria has been doing psychic readings and spiritual counseling for about seventeen years. During the past eight years she has been a guest on more than six thousand radio shows and has had her own interview talk show. She is a regular guest on more than forty radio stations throughout the United States and in Hong Kong, New Zealand, Australia, and the United Kingdom. She's developing a meditation audio-cassette tape, finishing her first book, and working on a syndicated radio show. To schedule a phone appointment, contact Victoria at (415) 978-9447 or toll-free at (888) 686-2200.

© 1998, Wayne Hudson, "A Koala and I Trusted Each Other."

© 1998, Ilona Goin, "A Conversation with the Brokenhearted Horse."

© 1998, Donald D. Reynolds, "The Grateful Wasp."

© 1998, Donna M. Lengyel, "Dillinger Teaches Me to Trust Again."

Chapter Eight: Recognizing Life's Mystical Moments

© 1995, Jelaluddin Rumi, "Birdsong from Inside the Egg," as quoted in *The Essential Rumi.*

© 1998, Allen Anderson, "Taylor's Blessing."

© 1998, Jan Warren, "Guardian Angel Bees." Jan Warren is a Super Blue-Green Algae distributor. The algae is wild, and she has found its ancient base of nutrition truly brings back life and vitality to herself and to animals. To contact Jan, call (800) 659-8055, ext. 11128.

© 1998, Linda Anderson, "The Elephant Learned to Fly."

© 1998, Jackie Gilson, "Molly's Miraculous Return." If you would like to donate to Molly's organization, Central California Labrador Retriever Rescue, send contributions to Jackie at 7889 E. Harney Lane, Lodi, CA 95420. Her web site is http://www.cc-labrescue.org.

© 1998, Karen Donaldson, "How a Stubborn Horse Saved Sam's Life." Karen Donaldson's book, *Haunted Houses of Michigan,* is available from Whitechapel Productions, Forsyth, IL.

© 1998, Bianca Rothschild, "The Quality of Mercy."

© 1997, Doreen Virtue, Ph.D., "The Sea Lion Who Taught Me the Power of Praying Together." Doreen is the author of *Divine Guidance* (Renaissance/St. Martin's, 1998) and *Angel Therapy.* She gives workshops across the country every weekend. For more information on Doreen's books or workshop schedule, call (800) 654-5126, ext. 0 or visit her Web site at http://www.AngelTherapy.com.

© 1998, Maryse Gauthier, "Pucette Found a Way to Say, 'Merci!' "

© 1998, Joyce Stoffers, "Eugene Finds a Home." Joyce is the managing editor of *Westview: A Journal of Western Oklahoma.*

Part Three: What Angel Animals Teach Us About Death, Dying, and the Afterlife

© 1996, Margot Lasher, *And the Animals Will Teach You: Discovering Ourselves Through Our Relationships with Animals*, The Berkley Publishing Group, 375 Hudson Street, New York, NY 10014, http://www.penguinputnam.com. Reprinted with permission.

Chapter Nine: Saying Good-bye in Our Own Way

© 1940, Rudyard Kipling, "Just So Stories—The Butterfly That Stamped," *Rudyard Kipling's Verse, Definitive Edition*, Doubleday and Company, Inc., Garden City, New York.

© 1998, Allen and Linda Anderson, "Saying Good-bye to Feisty."

© 1998, Maxine Wilson, "Deer at the Window."

© 1998, Bob Marshall, "A Guinea Pig Gave Me Precious Time with My Dying Father."

© 1998, Eleanor Jane Briest, "A Cat Let Me Know How Much I Meant to Him."

© 1997, Damaris Miller, "Dreaming My Farewell to Springer."

© 1998, Bradley Hill, "Willy Wouldn't Leave Until I Said Good-bye."

© 1998, Lisa Chewning, "Split Hearts in the Snow." Lisa Chewning teaches creative writing in a workshop program she has developed. For more information, contact Lisa at Write It Right, 368 Atlantic Avenue, Apt. G, Pittsburgh, PA 15224, (412) 401-5622.

© 1998, Mary Grady-Thorne, "Roma and the Dancing Black Bear Reassured Me."

Chapter Ten: Going Through Grieving

© 1995, Jeffrey Moussaieff Masson and Susan McCarthy, *When Elephants Weep: The Emotional Lives of Animals*, Delacorte Press, Bantam Doubleday Dell Publishing Group, Inc., 1540 Broadway, New York, NY 10036. Reprinted with permission.

© 1998, Mary Kate McKenna, "A Brokenhearted Mouse Taught Me About Grieving."

© 1998, Christina Louise Dicker, "The Quail Offered Hospice."

© 1998, Diane Robinson, "A Rabbit Showed That We Each Grieve in Our Own Way."

Chapter Eleven: Messages from Heaven

Chapter Twelve: Recognizing Angel Animals Who Return